The Enemies Within Us

a Memoir

Sharon A. Crawford

The Enemies Within Us
Copyright © 2020 Sharon A. Crawford
All rights reserved
Published by Blue Denim Press Inc.
First Edition
ISBN - 978-1-927882-58-0
No part of this book may be used or reproduced in any manner whatsoever without written permission except in the case of brief quotations embodied in critical articles or reviews.

This is a work of non-fiction. Fictional names have been used for everyone except for the author, her parents, and grandparents. See Disclaimer for more details.
Parts of this memoir were previously published in an essay by the author, "Don't Look Down," in the online publication *The Smart Set* in January 2019.

Cover Image—istock.com/ilze79
Cover Design—Shane Joseph/Typeset in Cambria and Garamond

Library and Archives Canada Cataloguing in Publication
Title: The enemies within us : a memoir / Sharon A. Crawford.
Names: Crawford, Sharon A., 1948- author.
Identifiers: Canadiana (print) 20200309609 | Canadiana (ebook) 20200309900 | ISBN 9781927882580

 (softcover) | ISBN 9781927882597 (Kindle) | ISBN 9781927882603 (EPUB)
Subjects: LCSH: Crawford, Sharon A., 1948—Childhood and youth. | LCSH: Crawford, Sharon A., 1948—

 Family. | CSH: Authors, Canadian (English)—21st century—Biography. | LCSH: Children of cancer patients—

 Biography. | LCSH: Catholic children—Biography. | LCGFT: Autobiographies.
Classification: LCC PS8605.R44 Z46 2020 | DDC C813/.6—dc23

Beware not the enemy from 'without' but the enemy from 'within.'
—**Douglas MacArthur**

Other Works by Sharon A. Crawford

Fire Underneath the Ice, a novella co-authored with Rene Natan under the name R.S. Natanevin, Rogue Phoenix Press, 2010

Beyond the Tripping Point, a collection of crime short stories, Blue Denim Press, 2012

Beyond Blood, a novel, Blue Denim Press, 2014

Beyond Faith, a novel, Blue Denim Press, 2017

Disclaimer

To protect the innocent, the guilty, and everybody else, most names have been changed and often only fictitious first names are used. However, I have used the real names for my parents, my beloved grandfather's first name, and for me. Although I refer to the house I grew up in as "139," without its exact address, all other street names, places and dates are real. Interactions between my parents and me, and with other family members, friends, colleagues, acquaintances etc., are as true as my memory recollects. I have taken a bit of liberty with dialogue as that is something you don't always remember word-for-word. But the actual connections that instigated the dialogue happened.

Dedication

Dedicated to all of my family past and present—Mom and Dad, my son Martin and his partner, Juni, grandparents, aunts, uncles, and cousins. Family—eccentric or not—defines who we are. We may not all have got along; we may still be in flux. But that is the nature of families. I have learned and continue to learn much from you and am grateful for knowing all of you.

Contents

Introduction 1

Prelude 3

Part One: Crashing Into Life 4

   1: A Home Is Not a House 5

   2: Practising Gardening and Religion 15

   3: Protecting the Princess 24

Part Two: Riding The Rails With Daddy And Mommy 32

   4: Riding the Rails with Daddy 33

   5: Destination Stateside 44

   6: Destination—Rural One 46

   7: Destination—Rural Two 54

   8: City Travels with Mom 63

   9: Destination—City Cousins 73

Part Three: The Hard Knocks Of Learning 77

   10: Mom's Eight Rules of Honesty 78

   11: Tales In and Out of Grade School 85

   12: The Enemy Within Starts Surfacing 96

Part Four: Living With Devastation 101

   13: Life Goes On? 102

   14: Don't Look Down—Ever 117

   15: Tales from the Grade Eight Crib 123

16: The Summer Between...131

17: Tales from the High School Bunker 135

18: Boys, Beatles, and the 15 to 20 Club 144

19: Boys, Girls, and Teachers..160

20: D is Also for Daddy 168

Part Five: Off To Work I Go 174

21: Hi Ho and All That Work Jazz 175

22: Seeing Through Blue-coloured Glasses 186

Part Six: Endings And Beginnings 192

23: Suddenly 193

24: The Road Most Travelled...208

Epilogue...215

Acknowledgements...216

Author Bio 218

Introduction

*Y*our *dad has cancer.*

Words that no little girl should ever have to hear.

Words that would eventually skewer my relationship with my daddy.

Especially if it was first kept secret.

Especially depending on who told you.

Words that would change my family's life forever.

Of course, it was not always that way for me, at least for the first 10 years. I grew up in what I call the grey ages—the 1950s to the late 1960s. As revealed in my memoir *The Enemies Within Us*, I had an abundance of other stuff to deal with. I was a shy only-child who worshipped authority—parental, religious, and teacher—and wanted to please others. Instead, I collided with two bullies—a friend and a nun. At that time, bullying was supposedly tamer by today's social media standards.

Daddy and Mommy were what used to be called elderly parents, especially Daddy, as he was old enough to sometimes be mistaken for my grandfather. Perhaps that had something to do with us being close. He referred to me as his little Princess, and he was my King who bailed me out of problems I had with others. Mom, however, tried to teach me to stand up for myself.

Thanks to Daddy's position as timekeeper for the Canadian National Railway, CNR, I became a railroad brat, riding the rails for free with Mommy and Daddy to visit her extensive, somewhat eccentric family, in southwestern Ontario and Detroit, Michigan. Daddy's family, also bordering on the eccentric, lived mainly in Toronto. The three of us did take a side-trip to New York City by train, of course, but on CPR, the rival railroad, because it had an overnight train. We slept sitting up.

However, a big shadow hung over my childhood, a shadow called "sickness and death." Just before my 10th birthday, it invaded my home, wearing an invisible big C on its chest, and silently following Mommy, Daddy, and me 24/7. Before that, I dreamt of fires and floods coming after us. The reality was much worst. Fires and floods don't begin with a "C." "Cancer" does.

With all this happening, I turned to writing— daily entries in diaries and poetry, then as an adult, a journalist who picked away at story ideas, interviewing people, and writing about them and their issues. I would ask them about their background, their childhood, and how it connected to who and what they became. Somewhere during that time period I began writing my memoir—several versions. It was shoved on the backburner when I started writing the Beyond murder mysteries with complicated plots. But I am also a writing instructor who teaches memoir writing. Listening to my students' stories in-the-works and helping them make their stories better, as well as writing my own short personal essays, reminded me of my own unfinished memoir.

So, the writer in me began digging, sifting, re-organizing, writing, and rewriting. As I dug deeper and deeper, I found help in a most unusual way…

… In my memoir, **The Enemies Within Us**, my present-day senior self meets my little-girl self. We join forces to tear apart what really happened growing up in Toronto, southwestern Ontario, Detroit, and New York City back in the 1950s, 1960s and early 1970s, especially when your Daddy "gets" cancer. To do this, we both contribute to the story. I invite you to walk backwards in time in *our* shoes—the little girl me and the senior me in **The Enemies Within Us**.

Prelude

There are nights when the wolves are silent and only the moon howls.
—**George Carlin,** US comedian and actor (1937—2008)

The wind whistles around me like an invisible avenger swooping down in the dark night. On this cold dry evening in early November 1957, I am squeezing Mommy's hand as we scurry home from Brownies along Lesmount Avenue in east end Toronto. I try to look straight ahead but can't help glancing to the left. The driveways are filled with murky shadows looming into human shapes that seem to leap towards me. I dig my nails into Mommy's hand. A streetlight pops like a camera flash, catching a maple tree shuddering, its winter branches stripped bare from its shield of summer leaves. I want to run home; I want to *be* home. But Mommy continues steering me in a steady, brisk walk.

Mommy and Daddy are supposed to guarantee *my* security, and our home is supposed to provide me sanctuary, but they are elderly parents. They *do* try in their own ways to help me, their only child.

But interior and exterior demons keep getting in the way. Demons like that knock on the front door in the middle of the night.

Part One: Crashing Into Life

Daddy and Toddler Sharon in Backyard of 139

Mom with Toddler Sharon in Backyard of 139

1: A Home Is Not a House

You Can't Go Home Again.
—Thomas Wolfe

One late night, loud pounding on the front door wakes Mom, Daddy, and me. Like the servant heeding the master, we all trip out to the front entrance. Mom turns on the veranda light and yanks the door open.

"Do you know this man?" A police officer stands on our veranda. His right hand supports the shoulder of a dishevelled man.

"Uh, home," the man says.

The stench of his breath assaults my nostrils, and I jump back behind Mom, then peek out. The man's oily black hair lies flat. Night shadow and red blotches compete for attention on his face. He is bare from his neck to his dark trousers. Looking closer, I see blood dribbling down from a deep slice on his left cheek onto his chest. His eyes look bloodshot and vague. A black lump swells above his left eye.

"Home?" he asks again.

"Sharon, go back to bed," Daddy says.

Fascinated and repulsed, I lean out a little further. Who is this man?

"Oh, dear Lord," my mother says. "It's Mr. Vargo from two doors down."

Not from here; our house is safe. Our house will protect us from harm. But can its bricks and mortar stop evil from hovering within?

Maybe we should have taken this knock on the door as a warning.

***

Our home, #139, a World War II-built bungalow, was located on a short road which ended at a cul-de-sac in Toronto's east end. That location should have nailed it as a big security blanket. But appearances can tell lies.

I was a scaredy-cat hiding behind Mommy's words and Daddy's protection. Daddy could do no wrong.

However, Daddy had one dirty little habit. He smoked. Day and night. Inside and outside the house, and probably at work. He had a ritual of making his own cigarettes in the basement, where mother banished him.

So, in the wisdom of my seven years, I sneak downstairs and pretend to play with Patsy and Darlene, my doll family, just to watch the ritual.

At the back of the unfinished basement, Daddy sits at his workbench just outside Mom's root cellar door. I drop Patsy and Darlene into their doll carriage, tiptoe towards Daddy, and peer over his shoulder. He turns around and smiles.

"Come here, Sharon. Want to see how it's done."

I sit down beside him and watch.

Hunched over his workbench, he resembles a shoemaker with all the materials of his trade spread out before him. Except he works with tobacco, not leather, and the faint smell of fresh unlit tobacco loiters in the vicinity of the workbench.

Daddy separates the wafers of white paper, placing one flat on the workbench. He reaches for an open tin of tobacco, and with his thumb and index finger, pinches a wad and sets it on the paper. He smooths it out almost to the edge and pushes it again until it resembles a thin line of dry roughage. With deliberate care, he picks up the paper's edge and starts rolling it with the tobacco inside. When he finishes, he licks one side. It is a cigarette. I think it is magic.

"Would you like to try rolling one?" he asks.

I nod and dig in, thick, clumsy kid fingers pushing fibre into the fine paper. My cigarettes would give you cancer just from looking at them. But I do more; I am helping my father make his own death. Of course, we don't know any better, then. The ritual of father and daughter rolling cigarettes brings me closer to him and gives me comfort.

So do other family customs.

Daddy was already grey-haired and old enough to be my grandfather when I arrived. I often wondered why it took my parents nine years to have children. When he married my mother in 1939, Daddy had already reached 40. Years later I learned from my cousin, Thelma, that he had a reputation as a "ladies man" before mother snagged him. In the Bloor and Bathurst Streets area, now Toronto's Annex, Daddy had earned the nickname, "Dapper Albert." He stood five foot three inches, with smoothed-back hair, once a sharp ebony, then a sleek grey, then white tufts mingled with bald patches.

A picture of Daddy and Mommy shows them with arms wrapped around each other's neck. Both are smiling. She wears a sloppy knit dress drooping below her knees, while he sports white shoes, a white shirt, sleeves rolled to the elbow, and a striped tie. The shirt billows slightly at his waist and his light pants have that pressed crease-down-the-middle look. His hair is grey, so it is probably some years after they were married. It is difficult to see a wedding ring on mother's finger. The picture isn't in colour, so everything comes across as shades of black, white, and grey. One thing sticks out in my father's right hand—the debonair 1940s and 1950s prop—a lit cigarette.

But not at this dinner table. Here Mommy and Daddy focus on leftovers from last evening's budget talk and leftovers on their plates. Daddy, however, also concentrates on another priority—his watch.

"Julia," Daddy says, as he scoops fried potatoes from his plate. "We can afford a rec room. We bought this house for $5,300, $500 down, $908.50 to close, two mortgages, and we paid it all off last year. So we can afford this."

I can't look at Daddy's or Mommy's face as I wait for her reply, so I stare at Daddy's arms—grey speckled hairs springing from the rolled-up shirt sleeves to the gold expansion watch.

"We had help," she says, and I turn to her, catching her smiling, thin lips spreading below a rather large nose. "We *need* help. *I* need help" will become her mantra a few years later.

Now Daddy starts commiserating with his watch, his eyes to-ing and fro-ing from his left arm to the wall clock.

"Albert," Julia says. "Do you have to do that during dinner?"

He continues lifting the watch and staring at its large face. I wait for the wide gold band to go "boing-boing," but the only sounds are the tick-tick of the wall clock, which Daddy regards as the God-of-all-time, and my mother exhaling her breath as she waits for an answer. I continue moving potatoes and peas around on my plate, but sneak a glance first over at Daddy and then Mommy.

"Have to take it into Riry Birk's to get it regulated," he says. "It's been three months since the last time I took it in."

I don't recall the rest of their conversation. Maybe they realize that "little ears" sits between them, but I guess my daddy wins, because soon the basement of our house undergoes a big upheaval, and I fast lose my tricycle-scooting area to wood planks and spare radiators.

***

When it came to getting things done around the house, if Mommy and Daddy couldn't do it themselves, they turned to friends and colleagues, such as Keith the singing plumber. When house pipes acted up, Keith arrived, and after he fixed the offending plumbing device, he let *his* pipes loose. He sang opera, loud and gregarious, not to the height of breaking the glass top of the door between the living room and front hall, but shattering any love on my part for the form.

One of Keith's colleagues was a carpenter, who became part of our Saturday life, banging away at two-by-fours downstairs, building a sub-floor, and nailing in the pine. Somehow, Mom started including him in our Saturday lunch. She did her down-in-the-kitchen deal—hot chicken noodle soup from a package, plates of white bread, Spam, a slab of hard margarine, iceberg lettuce, and maybe sliced cucumbers on the side. Mom and I would pull the kitchen table out from the wall, squeeze in the fourth chair behind, and make a big show to get everybody seated. After the scuffling of chairs, the slurping of chicken soup would compete for audio with the clock on the wall.

"Do you want some bread?" Mom asks as I watch. She passes the plate to the carpenter on her left.

"Thank you," he says.

The margarine follows, and he slops it on his bread. Unlike Daddy, he wears a wedding ring on his left finger and his arms sprout black hairs. A white pate crowns his head and smidgeons of black hair lie flat on either side. At least my daddy still has hair, albeit grey.

"How is your family?" Mom asks. She holds her soupspoon halfway to her mouth.

"Fine," the carpenter replies.

Slurp. Slurp. This time from Daddy. I start counting pieces of chicken in my soup.

After a few months, my mother is sick of playing restaurant.

"I can't keep making him lunch. Why doesn't he bring his own lunch?" she says to me as she opens the soup package. So, one Saturday, she sets only three places at the table, says nothing to Mr. Carpenter, and doesn't bother to call him to come up for lunch. It's just the three of us, gathered around the table.

"What else could I do?" Mom asks us. Her eyes plead for approval.

Daddy and I sit in silence and stare at our food. Each whack of the hammer shooting up from the basement seems to shout "coward," and I don't feel much like eating chicken soup. The following Saturday Mr. Carpenter arrives with a bagged lunch.

Saturday evenings, however, turn more personal. That's when the kitchen morphs into a prime war zone over who watches the black and white TV. The battle of the Perrys (Como and Mason) versus Foster Hewitt begins at the supper table.

"The hockey is on at 8 p.m.," Daddy says, glancing at his watch.

"I want to watch Perry Mason and then Perry Como," I say.

Mom likes the singing and detecting Perrys, so I know she'll side with me. After dinner, Daddy gives us the full performance, grunting as he unplugs the lime green radio from its place atop an older floor model in the living room. As he crosses the front hall, he stares at us, hurt look on his face, as if we robbed his soul. Then he thumps downstairs, and I hear a chair scraping on the floor. Mom closes the basement door. The smell of Daddy's cigarette smoke drifts up through the floorboards. When he comes upstairs to get another beer, the high sonorous voice of Foster Hewitt broadcasting the Toronto Maple Leafs playing the Montreal Canadians shoots through the open stairwell door. At this point, Daddy isn't speaking to us, and I worry it might be permanent and that scares me. Not knowing what to do, I just follow Mommy's silent direction—pretend not to notice; keep our eyes on the black and white TV screen and our mouths shut.

But the situation is only temporary. The radio is returned to the living room, and Daddy and I resume the close relationship of King Daddy and his little Princess. Besides, it wouldn't do to have war at Christmas—not in our house. And not for the first nine years of my life when Mommy and Daddy still believe in Santa Claus. When my best friend, The Bully, says, "Sharon, there's no Santa Claus," my mother goes into full defence mode.

"She's lying," Mommy says. "You've seen Santa at Eaton's. We leave raisin bread and milk for him on Christmas Eve, and aren't they gone in the morning?"

"Yes," I reply and hang onto my beliefs for another year. I know Santa doesn't bring everything under the tree. Can you see Santa, sitting down, fat protruding belly, fiddling with wrapping paper? Santa also doesn't bring the tree and he doesn't decorate it. That's *our* job.

When Daddy drags the Christmas tree into the house, I inhale the pine fragrance. It fills me with anticipation, prolonged as he attempts to fit the tree trunk into the stand.

"Get in there," he mutters between loud grunts and even louder bangs with the hammer. "Julia, can you hold onto the end for me?"

I can't watch the agony, so after Mom and I haul up the boxes of lights and ornaments from the basement, I sit in the kitchen, listening to the wall clock tick away. I hear "Jingle Bells" coming from the green radio. I peer inside the living room.

"Is it ready yet?" I ask.

"Patience," Mom says, handing Daddy a screwdriver.

"It's coming along." He twists the red tree stand. "Okay, Julia, let's push it up."

My parents heave the tree up to its majestic six feet, spreading dark green branches in the corner by the archway and brushing the mantle. Finally, I crouch down and dig into the box of ornaments.

"Wait a minute," Mom says. "The lights come first."

The two of them twine the lights throughout the tree, and I hold my breath one-two-three until I think I'll pop, as Daddy plugs in the lights and…

Nothing.

One light has burned out and the only way to find the culprit is to remove each light, one at a time, and try a light that might work. It is worse than waiting for Santa Claus. But when the miracle occurs, when the lights shine red, blue, white, yellow, and green, throughout the tree, Christmas leaps days closer.

Mom and I tackle the ornaments. I'm like a dog anxious for a walk, prancing around, reaching my paws down and up, and placing big coloured balls, small bells, and white plastic icicles on the sharp branches. Mom and I wrap tinsel– thin wavy strands and big gold bristles—which almost hide the lights, but they sparkle through. Then, I suck in my breath and look *way* up while Mom stands on the stepladder and places the angel in the top spot.

Mommy gives me a few dollars to buy Christmas gifts. Some go for Daddy's presents and some for Mommy's. Sometimes I need Daddy's help with the latter. One December, after checking out the local jewellery store, I drag Daddy in to look—not at jewellery—but at a ceramic wall decoration in white with red apples and purple plums painted on the front. He nods his approval and helps me pay for it.

The real joy of Christmas is wrapping the presents. A closed wooden door separates us—Mommy at the kitchen table and me at the dining room table. Amid the "pass the scotch tape; now keep your eyes shut," and the hurried covering of unwrapped presents, we could be wrapping side-by-side. I don't realize it then, but it is giving to someone I love that fills me with contentment. It doesn't matter that the fireplace is electric, or whether Santa exists, when Mommy and I wrap Christmas gifts, we are like one. Daddy never helps wrap presents, at least not when I am awake. He probably eats the raisin bread and drinks the milk left for Santa.

Then Christmas Day arrives. Like all good Catholics, we combine the secular and the religious…

I was awakened at about 7:40, and climbed out of bed, anticipating great joy and happiness. I dressed and "dumped" the contents out of my stocking. Then mom, dad, and I "dashed off" to Mass. We had expected Father T. to say Mass, but the pastor, Father M. did, instead. He is slow, to say the least, and he even preached a long sermon, and on Christmas, too. It was so hot in church. When we returned home, a woman banged on the door and started off on a spiel about it being a nice day. Then she went on about some literature she was selling. Mom cut her off short by banging the door in her face. Imagine peddling anything on Christmas of all days.

Christmas morning, 1963, Sharon's diary excerpt

Once back inside the house, it is open-the-presents time. Mommy and I sit on the chesterfield, leaving the pink easy chair for Daddy. It is my job to crawl under the tree and haul out the gifts. I make a point to find something with Daddy's name on it and "Love Sharon." Even at ages seven and eight I know there are less presents for him and don't want him to feel left out. I want to see his reaction to something I chose for him and bought with my own money given to me by Mommy. Not just a tie or socks, which despite my name on the card, she bought. Even if it is only a pen, it is *my* gift to him. He rips it open. No hugs, but a smile and a thank you.

"Just what I need," he says.

Once we have finished with the wrapped presents, Mommy, sometimes with Daddy helping, silently leaves the room, returning with my present from Santa.

A doll. I am dancing all over the living room, through the tossed wrapping paper on the floor and shouting "Thank you, thank you, Santa." At this point it isn't clear who I am really thanking—"Santa" or "Daddy."

After that first big day, Mom, Daddy, and I take over from Santa and the baby Jesus for New Year's Eve. Our job is to help the old year on its way out to yesterday's pasture and welcome the new year's arrival. We alternate with our friends, the Armsteads, from across the street to supply the venue. So, every-other New Year's Eve, our living room and dining room are filled with clinking glasses, low chatter, and the near-midnight snack served on the dining room table. Earlier in the day, Mom whirls through her cleaning frenzy, vacuuming two or three months' collection of dust bunnies hiding under the furniture, and denuding the dining room tabletop of its usual sewing paraphernalia, moving it all to the master bedroom—onto chairs, the floor closet, wherever she can find a spot. The big upright piano in all its pink roxatone glory remains under the window kitty-corner to the china cabinet, the latter donated by my godmother and her first husband and stained dark brown by Daddy. It is the only piece of furniture he ever stained, although I don't remember him actually doing it—no smells and no noise of sanding. Just the before and after. Yet, I can remember him rolling cigarettes. Today, I realize that was because the cabinet was for my mother's good dishes and the cigarette-making was a combined effort by Daddy and me.

Once the house is in order, Gerald and Marion Armstead, with their spinster daughter Ellen, drop over to visit. Mommy lets me stay up late. I half listen to the drone and whisper (one year, mother had laryngitis) while keeping an eye on the TV in the corner and the other eye (and stomach) focusing on the spread in the next room—delicate sandwiches filled with egg salad or salmon, minus the crusts now banished to the pop-up garbage can in the kitchen. When Mommy finally gives the "come and eat," signal, I stuff my pre-teen body with a midnight meal, while grabbing looks at *The Bells of St. Mary's* on TV. Warm room, congenial conversation, and the midnight feast lull me into a cocoon of false security.

A few years later, the day before the Armsteads move to an apartment, Marion Armstead will keel over and die from a heart attack. Many years later, their old house will blow up because of the feuding tenants. The basement tenant will screw around with the gas connection and late one weekday afternoon, *poof*. The teenage son, living upstairs with his parents, will miss the excitement by half an hour. His parents will be at work.

Our house doesn't blow up, but Daddy often throws his cigarette butts into the garbage can inside the garage. One Sunday afternoon, I'm looking out my bedroom window and I see smoke swirling from the garage. "Call the fire department," I yell out the window, but my daddy is quick on the mark, yanking open the garage door, hauling out the garbage can, and to my horror, stomping his foot inside. But he kills the fireworks.

"Don't worry. It's not serious enough to call the fire department." He smiles up at me.

When I go outside to investigate further, I discover the can also contains remnants of grass clippings.

I used to dream about fires when I was four or five years old. I would lie on my stomach in bed and see our house toppling in flames as Mom, Daddy, and I scurried around, collecting bits of our belongings, but I always woke up before I knew whether we got out safely.

Probably not, considering the unwelcome house guest we would harbour in a few years.

2: Practising Gardening and Religion

I hope that while so many people are out smelling the flowers, someone is taking the time to plant some.

—Herbert Rappaport [1]

During the night, two short figures sneak over the back fence into my mother's garden. Despite the dark, they seem to know where to go, crouching down and heading straight for a bushy patch. They drop to their knees, yank at a branch, break off something small and red, then shove it into their mouths. Perhaps one or both of them takes a tumble into the bushes. I'm fast asleep, so I don't know. But mother knows, and after years of keeping her opinions within our house, she will sit down at the phone in the dining room, and prepare to call the police.

...The family that plants together stays together...

Each April, when the first tulip showed its face in the flowerbed under the living room window, Mom *had* to get out in her garden and do her vegetable, fruit, and flower business. Mom and I moved in tandem with the garden and with religion, finding parallels. Both had beauty, filled us with awe, and brought order and ritual to our lives: plant seeds in spring and be rewarded with beautiful flowers, bountiful vegetables, and fruit in summer; go to Mass and Communion on Sunday and be rewarded in life with only good. What did I, a little girl, know about religion except what I heard and absorbed from the priests and nuns?

---

[1] Author of *Marking Time, How Our Personalities, Our Problems and Their Treatment Are Shaped By Our Anxiety About Time*, New York, 1990, Simon & Schuster, 1990.

Perhaps I should have fine-tuned my radar to Daddy. He was a player in both gardening and religion, but seemed to operate a few degrees off from Mom and me. Then I might have caught a whiff of his looming cancer—from the garden flowers, from the church incense.

On this particular April morning, however, the three of us appear to be in step. Mom thrusts her shovel, no-nonsense style, into the soft sand. Her black oxfords sink deep and the once-white socks are splattered with sand. She hides her body under a flowered housedress. Having a baby at 41 and the indignities and intricacies of middle age have remodelled her into Frau Frump. Nearby Daddy works another shovel, moving closer to clumps of small plants. I dig in with my tiny shovel, but make only small dents compared to their efforts. Mostly, I hover, watch, and listen.

"Albert," Mom says. "Be careful around the strawberry plants."

You can't blame her for taking precautions when digging. She is always complaining to Daddy and me that the berry population seems to diminish overnight even when she hasn't picked any. The remains not present the next day don't add up to a hungry posse of black birds or sparrows.

Finally, the planting begins. My clumsy digits bury the tiny radish seeds in the row of sand, which my mother carefully indents using the rake handle. When she hauls out the bean seed packet, she has her instructions ready.

"This is the top of the bean." She pats it with her index finger. "See, it's curved in. That's where the bean plant will sprout. You plant that part up or the bean will grow down."

I swallow my impatience and become the obedient daughter—please the parent and the world will bow to you. I have much to learn, but young age and the results of my gardening inexperience can excuse my naïve life expectations. The beans usually grow up, up towards the heavens, if you believe in fairy tales like Jack and the Beanstalk.

…*The family that prays together stays together*…

When I planted seeds in my mother's garden, when she still *had* a garden, I believed in religious stories. I tagged along to church with her and

Daddy. I liked the rich Greek *Kyrie Eleison* and Latin *Dominus Vobiscum*, sung while the soothing scent of incense filled the dark interior of the new Holy Cross Church, just like the fragrant flowers filling my mother's garden. This church opened December 12, 1948, eleven days after my birth. Something in this proximity of dates must have joined my soul with this small homey building because often in stressful times I sought sanctuary within its walls. Musty wood pews, sunlight peeking through stained glass windows, and the quiet would calm my insides, temporarily, provided that I avoided the dingy dark confessionals in the back. Even after moving away, in person and spirit, I would always return. I, who later tossed Catholicism and organized religion to the compost pile, would still march into the church for a family funeral and to reconnect with childhood parishioners.

Unlike Mom, Daddy takes church very casually—he attends Sunday Mass, but he stops at taking weekly communion.

"Communion is for Christmas and Easter," he says.

So Sunday morning early, I wake up in my bed, not to the smell of coffee, but to a commotion reverberating from the front of the house.

"Get out of here. Come on. Come on." Mother's voice shoots from the kitchen through the closed doors of the hallway and two bedrooms. Daddy and I aren't the recipients. Mom is yelling at a pot roast rebelling against her tugging it out of the undersized freezer above the refrigerator. I hear water running and metal clamping shut, then the smell of fresh coffee wafts into my bedroom. Two minutes later, Mom bangs on my door and opens it.

"Time to get up."

After my First Communion at age six, hurrying is a must if I want to eat breakfast before church. According to the rules back then, you must eat no later than one hour before Mass. Why? You don't go swimming at church, at least not at Holy Cross Catholic Church, so stomach cramps aren't a possibility. My friend, Nora, who skips breakfast, sometimes faints en route to the communion rail. So I drag my body up early to feed it before I feed my spirit.

Then it is off to church for Mom, Daddy and me. When we don't get a ride from the Cooks or the Kents, we walk the 15 minutes each way. In the summer, we parade down our street, Daddy leading in his lightweight beige suit (no tie), short-sleeved white shirt, and white shoes. Mom follows in her glorified housedress, nylon seamed stockings, chunky white oxfords, and straw hat, and with a hand in Mom's, me, in a flowered dress, white socks, flat white shoes, and straw hat. When we reach the busy street, we turn the corner. Then Daddy stops. We do not want to board a bus. We have to cross this busy street *in the middle between the street with lights and our street with no lights.*

"Wait a minute," Daddy says, looking left and right.

Once no cars are within running distance, he leads the parade out onto the road. I am terrified. He is there protecting us, but what if a car should careen around the corner? I can't look at him or check the street left and right. Instead, I clutch Mom's hand tighter as we scurry across. When not with Daddy, I can't cross the street without the lights, so I walk the extra blocks to the crosswalk just to avoid getting hit by a car. Little do I know that years later a car will indeed hit one of my play friends when she darts out between side streets onto the busy road.

…The family that plays together and prays together with friends stays together…

Although Mommy followed Daddy across traffic-laden streets, after church duty, she seldom followed the rule of "on the seventh day, rest." She *must* get into the garden. Despite the large vegetable and fruit patch, her Achilles heel was her roses.

The rosebushes spread everywhere—front, back, and if Mom could nurture roses through asphalt, the driveway would no doubt harbour a rosebush. Below the veranda, in the corner by the driveway, Mom has installed a small trellis. When I sprawl in the green Muskoka chair on the veranda, my nose inhales the intoxicating aroma of the yellow roses.

In the 1950s, we could hold a small wedding in our backyard at 139. The deep red roses climb and entwine around the white archway attached to the white picket fence beside the driveway. As I yank open the gate, the fragrance overwhelms me. My eyes absorb the colour, and while skipping through the backyard, I count the rosebushes winding around several trellises — against the back of the house, the side of our garage, and the neighbour's garage. Mother's roses grow high and their scent permeates my nose, skin and right into the core of my heart and soul. She constantly frets over a hybrid tea whose blossom colour exemplifies the species name. I don't recall the actual name of the rose, just Mom standing by the fence and fingering the petals.

"The leaves have too much blackspot," she says. "And this rose is finished." Snip, snip, then, "Oh, good morning, Mr. Swan."

I stand beside my mother and nod a "hello" to Mr. Swan. Old, heavyset, and banished outside by his wife so he can smoke, he stands silent like a sentinel in his driveway on the other side of the fence. Between puffs on his cigar, he nods and continues to stare at us. He is like a harbinger of what will come on our side of the fence. He gives me the creeps. I stick my nose in the rosebush, but all the sweet flowers in the world won't overpower the cancer connection with smoking. The multiple rosebushes and the other scented bushes seem like a rectangle of protection my mother's subconscious dredged up. However, smelling the flowers will not keep the black spot from attacking my daddy's lungs and brain. Why are daffodil sales used to collect funds for cancer research? If it is their colour, yellow, supposedly the colour of healing, then I can tell these researchers that it won't work. Although yellow is the colour of the radiant sun, the yellow roses, forsythia tree, and tulips my mother grows don't keep cancer at bay. When I combine the paltry results of my mother's tulip-bulb planting, the life cycle of the forsythia (yellow flowers first, leaves second), the roses (red, rose, pink, white, and yellow), maybe mother's garden is sprinkled with omens of the disease and its future colours of hope. Certainly, the causes of cancer permeate throughout—the neighbour's cigars and the cigarette and pipe smoke my daddy inhales and exhales. As a garden grows based on what you put into the soil, so can cancer grow from what you (or your environment) put inside your body.

Of course, we don't know that then.

If mother had killed the rosebush flaunting the black spot, would that have killed the cancer inside Daddy? Probably not. Rosebushes resemble life—bundled with thorns. And many of Mom's rosebushes lived blackspot free.

Daddy, however, had no problem deciding his priority among the shrubs. Instead of rose bushes, he focused on the non-thorny shrubs, especially when my friends and I removed some of their parts.

In the summer, my girlfriends and I play outside with our dolls. Give us green grass and trees, or at least big shrubs, and we are happy. We spread our blankets on the backyard grass, sit our dolls on top, stand up the open doll suitcases for a wall and hang their clothes inside. Then we set out our dolls' dishes and go hunt for dinner.

The raspberries, strawberries and tomatoes in mother's garden don't interest us. We are after the big green. Marie grabs a branch from the snowball tree over by the Swans' garage, and, one-by-one, picks off large velvety leaves. Dorothy, Jan, and I do the same and arrange the leaves on our doll plates. We pull some of the sharp pin leaves from the two small evergreens behind the house. We are just sitting down to dinner with our dolls, when Daddy comes through the archway. His stroll turns into a leap of rage.

"What are you girls doing? Stop picking the leaves." His face is red, and if he doesn't slow down he'll vault over the fence into the Swans' driveway.

The four of us stare at him, our mouths suspended open.

"Don't you know that you are hurting the trees?" he asks.

"Sorry, we didn't know," Marie says.

I say nothing. What's up with Daddy? We have to feed our dolls. However, our dolls' food now seems like poison.

That evening after dinner, Daddy hauls out the lawn mower and starts pushing it along the front lawn. I step out onto the veranda, but stay back, still reeling from the afternoon. Daddy catches me watching him, stops and beckons to me.

"Do you want to try it?" His voice sounds like the normal Daddy.

I must have nodded, because he invites me over to the mower and patiently explains how it works. First, he helps me steer it, then lets go. Pushing is heavy work on my own, but I shove it forward, and at his instruction and encouragement, move it around to return to our starting point.

Years later, when electric and gas mowers replace the manual, I will let my husband, then my son, cut the lawn with the gas mower. Later, I will give a few stabs at using an electric mower, but after it dies, I will buy a manual mower and cut my lawn just like Daddy did.

But the day after Daddy's scolding, my friends and I play over at Dorothy's where the tree pickings are slim and the lawn is lush. We pretend it is Sunday and dress our dolls for church. As the only Catholic, I am filled with righteousness. Dorothy and I tussle over whose religion reigns superior.

"Only Catholics go to heaven," I say.

"That's a lie," Dorothy says. She is Protestant, but her mom, a lapsed Catholic, married her dad, a divorced man, a big no-no in the Catholic Church.

"'Tis not. We learned that in catechism class." I frown at Dorothy.

"Not true."

"Yes, it is."

We are fast reaching the prelude to raising fists when Dorothy's father charges out and sends me home.

Home where Mom keeps busy with her vegetable and fruit garden and drags me into the process, complete with all the unknown dangers lurking inside and outside.

One August day, Mom comes in the side door from the garden. She is carrying an open tomato juice can and she is almost scowling.

"Sharon," she calls as I stand at the top of the stairway. "Have a look."

Not knowing what to expect, I hurry down and join her at the door. I lean forward, my nose almost touching the can when Mom reaches inside and hauls out a wiggling creature, a mini-Martian with aerials and a big, ugly body, green mixed with white and black. I jump back before it can attack me.

"Green hornworms," Mom says. "They won't bite, but they will gobble up all the tomato leaves, and then the tomatoes won't have anything to hang onto because the branches will collapse. Sharon, they won't hurt you." She shoves the tin closer to my frozen face. This time I just want it all to go away; I want to run up the stairs, but I can't tear my eyes away from these creatures. So, I move closer and stare again into the can and the squirming critters within. Mom shrugs, turns around, and takes the can of wrigglers outside. I peek through the screen door at the same time she turns around again.

Is she smiling? What's so funny? Those little monsters are worse than the blackspot on Mommy's roses. I'm glad she is taking them away from the house. The house must be kept safe. We must be kept safe.

I don't get it. I am still too young to realize that sometimes evil grows from within.

When not battling hornworms, Mom tackles her raspberry bushes gone wild, down the other neighbour's side of the garden and behind our garage. These bushes are ready to tango with the hedge that divides the garden from the lawn. Mom marches out with the pruning shears and cuts branches in snips and starts.

"They're getting all over the place," she mumbles. Snip. Snip.

I watch in bewilderment with no idea how she decides. She just *knows*.

This *just knowing* seemed to filter into religion, although it wasn't knowing all the answers, but knowing that if we believed in God and the Catholic Church, and absorbed all the rules, we would be rewarded in the next life, something too far off for a little girl's understanding. So, I learned rules of religion and garden, and tried to practice them, mostly by doing what I was told. Like when I helped Mom with canning the fruits and vegetables.

My favourite was the rhubarb strawberry mixture which Mom (with my help stirring and eating) boiled on the stove. Sometimes the mixture made it into a pie, sometimes jam. Often Mom, Daddy and I just ate the boiled mixture, as is, for several desserts. Unfortunately, not all the fresh fruit came from our garden. Thanks to the strawberry thieves, Mom had to supplement her strawberry supplies with store-bought, usually from a small vegetable and fruit shop.

At least these strawberries mixed with the rhubarb didn't get into the hands of the backyard robbers. Two of the boys living in the house behind us, including Tom in my class who defended me against The Bully, stole the strawberries, or so mother claimed..

But she never called the police. She didn't say why. Perhaps the reason was because she never caught them in the act. Years later, when Tom and I reconnect, he will admit to the crime.

The rituals and rewards of gardening and religion will soon lose their rhythms with us. The outside world will shovel its way inside; the invisible enemy lurking within will surface above ground, both of them combining to steal more than strawberries from our family. For many years, my gardening will manifest as potted plants only, and any religion will appear merely when necessary to save face.

Practising gardening and religion will finally teach me something about expectations.

3: Protecting the Princess

Parents can only give good advice or put children on the right paths, but the final forming of a person's character lies in his or her own hands.

—**Anne Frank**

I am learning to ride my bike, steering it past 139 and onto the dead-end street. It is exhilarating and somewhat scary. But I have an anchor—Daddy, hanging onto one handlebar and seat post, keeping me balanced, so I shouldn't fall off. Right?

Winter and summer he steered me through the obstacles of childhood play. Maybe his age made him do it. Perhaps he was just the doting dad. He was the King, and if he could help it, no one and nothing would ever hurt me. Mom, on the other hand, took a more practical, albeit sometimes skewed, approach. Maybe it was their differing backgrounds –country mouse (Mom) and city mouse (Daddy) colliding. Mom was born on a farm near Mildmay, Ontario and didn't move to Toronto until obtaining secretarial work there in her 20s. Daddy was French-Canadian and was born in Montreal. The Langevin family moved to Toronto when my father was a child.

The two did collaborate once, when my sixth birthday rolled around. That's when they decided I needed to learn to ice skate. As my oddball elderly parents, they had to put their own personal twist on the teaching process. So, Daddy constructed the ice rink, and Mommy got me moving on it.

Daddy turns on the hose, and out pours cold water. Overnight it freezes on the dormant grass in the backyard. I never think how the water passes through the hose. Wouldn't it be frozen? Does Daddy put his ear to the lime green radio and listen to the weather reports to see when the daytime temperature sits around freezing (32 degrees Fahrenheit then) or just below? When night falls, so does the temperature, and in the morning—magic—instant skating rink.

Then Daddy turns it over to Mommy. Like a dance instructor trying to teach steps to a nervous wannabe, she grabs my hands and tries to set me in motion.

"Come on Sharon. Just slide your feet, one foot in front of the other."

My feet, tucked tightly into new white figure skates, scrape and totter along the ice and my fingers dig into her hands; her mittens no protection for the hard, petrified squeeze I give her. I do not want to fall. I might break a leg. I'm terrified of losing control, so carry on clinging to Mom as she steps backward, sometimes in her rubber boots and sometimes in an old pair of Daddy's black hockey skates. I follow forward like a drunken clown.

Two winters of this private slide and lurch pass by. Then my eighth birthday arrives. "You're ready for Dieppe Park," Mom says.

The big time. Dieppe Park has two enclosed hockey rinks and one large pleasure skating rink. Mom and I walk down Greenwood and along Cosburn Avenue. When we arrive, Mom takes me into the cold changing room. She assists me as I shiver into extra socks and the skates; then she laces them up.

"Is this tight enough?" she asks. "Better make it tighter." She pulls on the laces until I think my ankle will stay straighter than a lamppost.

Then she hands me the skate guards, which I grab with my left hand; my right hand takes hers and I push my bum forward. I try to imagine I am standing but it seems strange and impossible. But I get up. It feels as if I am balancing on stilts the width of a sliver and the weight of a brick. This is not the way I want to see the world better, and I imagine that the world's eyes are staring at me as Mom walks, and I teeter out the door into colder cold. When we arrive near the ice, my left ankle starts to wobble.

"Sit down here, and I'll fix it." Mom points to the bench.

I grip the seat and, like Frankenstein's monster, plop down. Mom unlaces the offending skate, purses her lips, grunts, and yanks on the laces.

If my lungs were in my ankle I would suffocate. She reaches the top of the skate and ties the laces into a bow, followed by a knot.

Then she turns me loose.

I clutch the skate guards, one in each hand, and stagger slowly. Surrounding me are people—old, young, even a few boys wielding hockey sticks. Aren't they supposed to be on the hockey rinks? I take a cautious step onto the ice and almost lose my footing, so I point one skate guard out to find some balance, then put one foot in front of the other, hold both skate guards out, and I'm off.

It is exciting, and a little frightening, but I am skating around the rectangular rink. No one can call me stupid now. I am gliding and… a hockey-wielding teenage boy nearly crashes into me as he takes the corner too fast. I clutch the skate guards and skate on the spot. Then I get my momentum. Yippee. I can skate. I will continue skating outings until my late 20s—always clutching the skate guards.

Come spring a year and a half later, I am nine years old and learning to ride my bike. I cycle past 139, onto the dead-end street. Daddy is steering me. We do this almost daily after he comes home from work.

Daddy shows great patience teaching me to ride my bicycle. I am a late bloomer to this sport. In sneakers, white socks, pink pedal pushers, and a sleeveless cotton blouse, topped by a face showing clenched teeth, this princess perches on her narrow throne, 28 inches off the road. Trying to keep my balance on two wheels and navigate the whole thing forward scares me.

"You can do it," Daddy says. He hangs onto the left handlebar and the seat post while walking with me down the street, as I learn to keep the soles of my shoes on the pedals and my heart inside my chest. Then The Bully rides by on her bike. No father holds her up and steers her.

"Hi," she says as she zooms by. Later, it is, "You can't even ride a bike. You have to get your dad to push you."

The Bully is my childhood nemesis. She is two weeks older than me, and during part of my childhood she lives around the corner. We met just before beginning grade school. Because she and I would be walking to kindergarten with the same 11-year-old girl, Mary, Mrs. Bully and Mom decided their daughters should meet beforehand.

The Bully's mom comes around and introduces her daughter. Mrs. Bully knocks on the side door and says "hello." I stand in my usual spot, at the top of the inside stairs and cower behind Mom's flowered skirt. But I peek. Outside the screen door, standing straight and short is this four and three-quarters-year-old girl with clipped mousey hair and an impish grin.

I dart back behind Mom's skirt.

She, of course, is her usual sociable self. I don't know it then, but Mom and Mrs. Bully are friends from a few years back who will share the ups, downs, and in-betweens of parenthood. Occasionally, Mom will let some of their secrets slide out, but it won't be until after the Bully family moves away that she'll tell me why The Bully wanted me gone. It is only natural that if the mothers bond, so should the daughters. But that bond is not "friends for life;" it soon morphs into torture and tease with a dollop of glue. Mom and Daddy both have to extricate me from The Bully's clutches. Like politicians at election time, they don't approach the situations in tandem.

When The Bully and her gang chase my friend Dorothy and me down the street, Daddy dons his invisible king cloak and crown, and charges forward with his authority. But not before some damage is done.

The Bully Gang—Vera, Marie, Shannon (The Bully's younger sister by two years), and The Bully—line themselves against Dorothy and me. They chase us up and down the street. Dorothy and I run, hearts pounding, breath hitting high notes with the fear factor shuddering through our bodies. We spiral around in circles into the Harmon front yard, onto the street, back to the yard. Dorothy and I chase them into the backyhard. Vera slams the gate shut against us. A mistake on her part because Dorothy and I now have the edge on them as they are stuck in an enclosed area.

However, they are jumping up and down, and through the steel gate, yelling, "Nah. Nah, Nah." I am rolling on a high, and nothing and no one can stop me. I pick up a fist-sized rock from the ground, glare at them, and squeeze the rock as if it is my new best friend. You're in for it, Bully. I raise my arm over the gate and throw the rock… smack into Marie's forehead.

No. No. Not Marie. I like Marie. I can't understand why she's joined up with The Bully. I stand still and shocked. We seem lost in this sudden limbo second. The rock falls to the grass, and we jolt into screamland.

Then the Bully Gang opens the gate and breaks free.

"You're in for it," they say. "We're gonna get you now."

Dorothy and I turn and fly towards my place. The Bully Gang is a posse on our tail. Daddy, on holidays from work, leads Dorothy and me downstairs. He locks the side door for our safety. I turn to the basement window. Outside, The Bully and her followers shake their heads and waggle their hands. Then The Bully flattens her face against the window, and ugly intent and uglier expressions mesh into what could pass as roadkill. I shiver and turn to Dorothy. If we looked in a mirror, our faces would show us resembling twins. We back away, and I wish Mommy had made curtains for the window. But there is no bright light, no feeling of freedom in running around inside a then unfinished basement with its white cement pillars and tarred concrete floors. Dorothy and I are the victims. Why are we the ones confined inside?

Mommy uses subtler tactics. How else to explain our silent collusion when one day The Bully and I get into it with words?

I don't remember the issue, but we're standing outside on my front veranda. The Bully is letting me have it; I am burning hotter and hotter inside. Mommy must hear us because when I run inside to get a knife, she hands me a ruler. The Bully knows she's in trouble and she runs down the steps. Brandishing the ruler like I'm Zorro without the mask, I tear after her down the stairs, down the street, and around the corner. I'm steaming with how good it will feel to whack her one across the back and head, but she is too far ahead of me. Unlike Zorro, I have no horse, only my short eight-year-old legs. After she dashes inside, I land at the side door of her house, shake my ruler, and yell through the screen door. Too bad I lack any nerve to run into her house and finish the job, but what will her mother think and do?

Maybe Mommy is trying to protect me by teaching me to stand up for myself.

That summer The Bully convinces every kid on the block that I'm a witch. We're playing a game of *Chase the Witch* in the middle of the street outside 139, and the whole gang comes after me.

"Witch, witch," they say as they surround me.

I am the discard, the sacrifice, and their chanting shoots from my ears into my heart. I close my eyes and see flames, and the leaping gang ready to throw me in. Where are Mommy and Daddy now? I wish Daddy would charge out of the house, chase this screaming mob away, and take me downstairs inside the house. I promise I will not complain about the lack of curtains. But Daddy is still at work. Mommy is inside the house, with the doors and windows closed to keep out the summer heat.

There is no escape. The gang will burn me at the stake.

Then I open my eyes and see the girls who are supposed to be my friends still dancing around me. No visible flames, only the hot sun beating down on us.

"Witch, witch. Sharon is a witch," they continue to chant.

"Be gone," I want to say. I am too frightened.

The heat saves me. The girls wind down, probably worn out from their exercise in the sun, and all is quiet.

On another day Mommy does come to the rescue. The Bully's youngest sister, Katie, decides she wants to be my best friend and starts hanging around on my veranda. Although it is my job to go inside and dry the dishes after lunch, Mommy's call to action never comes. Later after Katie leaves, Mommy steps outside.

"You need to have one friend," she says. "That's why I let you play instead of calling you in to dry the dishes."

She must know that the others treat me like a pariah. On sunny summer mornings, she parks me outside with my colouring book and crayons at the card table on the front veranda. I sit there in the slowly receding shade from the house and carefully pick out crayons to colour in the trees, flowers, people, and cartoon characters of my vast colouring book collection. Boxes holding only eight crayons are not good enough; I need at least 24 crayons because then I can pick out different browns for the hair and different greens for the grass and trees. I pull out a crayon, lift it to my nose to inhale the waxy smell, then apply it to the drawings of people and places. I make sure my crayon stays within the outline and that I shade evenly. No wisps or coloured lines scattered all over the page. Already I am realizing that I need some order in my life. But not without the spontaneous sweetness of nature. Often, I lift my head from colouring to stare at the green grass and trees along the block and listen to the birds tweeting. Occasionally, a neighbour strolls by. We don't wave or say "hello," but I sense the peacefulness, not just between us, but overall. The neighbourhood is quiet now, and I need to absorb this. It is more than just breathing—it is my reboot into living after confrontations with The Bully. Of course, I don't figure this all out then. I am just content to soak up the moment without any angry outbursts.

I know now that Mommy sensed this need, and this was her way of getting me back in gear. Perhaps she realized that because I had no brothers or sisters, I had to go it alone. Perhaps she felt guilty because she and Daddy had not "given" me a sibling.

But other situations had been brewing on my street.

"A man was killed there in the road," I hear Mommy whisper to Daddy.

When she sees "little ears" standing nearby, she shuts her mouth and smiles. This is no conversation for a child. I peek out the living room window. The road is a mess of bulldozers, pneumatic drills, dirt, a street-length hole, and men climbing in and out of it. Complete chaos. It scares me.

"The city is digging up the street to put in new sewer pipes," Mom says. "You will have to play inside or in the backyard."

The man who died was one of the construction workers; he died in the hole. I don't recall if he had a heart attack or if it was an accident; I didn't see it happen. But every time Mommy opens the inside door to let in fresh air, I get a closer look at the construction shambles than the window view provides, with the bonus of unwanted noise barging in. For some reason my childish mind connects the man who died with the father of a friend, Gary, down the street. Gary's father did die, but later when I was a teenager, so he wasn't the unfortunate in the construction death.

What was and is unfortunate are the peripherals of Daddy's cancer, those little things that grow out of the situation and return to haunt you. After Daddy will begin battling cancer, distant cousins, and aunts and uncles will tell me that he used to be so proud of me. He would hold my hand and walk me down the street. I remember my *mother* pushing me in my stroller along O'Connor, past the park where I would later swing sky high on the swings. I can still feel the sensation of sitting close to the sidewalk while the stroller seemed to move under my feet and bum. To a three-year-old it was an exciting ride, held safe by the confines of the buggy and Mom's protective hold on it. But Daddy walking with me and pushing it? I drew a blank when reminded of this in my teens and I draw a blank now. I have to look at an actual photo of me, at age two, stuffed into a snowsuit sitting in the stroller in front of the veranda. Standing behind and resembling a prominent businessman in his dark heavy winter coat and Fedora, is my Daddy. His hands do not hold a briefcase, but rest on the stroller handles.

They say cancer changes your life, your family, and the connections between. I would soon find that out. However, first, I had to get to know my family, including my many aunts, uncles, and cousins. It would be a strange ride. But which was weirder—the journey to them? Or my family and the journey with them?

Part Two: Riding The Rails With Daddy And Mommy

CNR 1950s Railway Coach Exhibited Mildmay 2004

Grandpa Charlie's Farmhouse Two Miles from Mildmay

4: Riding the Rails with Daddy

Oh! Do not attack me with your watch. A watch is always too fast or too slow. I cannot be dictated to by a watch.
—**Jane Austen,** (1775—1817), *Mansfield Park*

If you're going to travel on the train with Albert Langevin, be prepared to get up early and arrive at the station long before the steam engine is fired up, long before the conductor and trainman arrive, and long before anyone else stands in line at Platform 9 for Guelph, Ontario. My daddy has to be first in line at Toronto's Union Station. His "typical CNR" style dictated our family schedule during the late 1950s and early 1960s when we travelled by train to Grandpa's and my godmother's farms, and to cities south of the Canada/US border.

What did I expect when Daddy had been working as a railway timekeeper since 1918?

On the way to Union Station, Daddy sits in the front seat of the taxi. Mom and I, with my doll Darlene, sit in the back.

"The best way to get to Union Station," Daddy says, looking down at his watch, "is to take Broadview down to Eastern Avenue, then take Eastern Avenue to Front Street." He scowls over at the driver. "We don't want to miss our train."

Not likely. Unless we get stuck in traffic on this pre-Don Valley Parkway day in the late 1950s, we will arrive an hour and a half early at Union Station.

The driver makes a right turn, and Daddy jumps into attack mode.

"I said to take Broadview to Eastern. We're on Gerrard Street now. Turn left at Parliament and go down Parliament to Front Street." Daddy removes his watch and is practically shaking it at the driver.

I don't need all this fuss as I'm trying to avoid getting carsick. Mommy and Daddy don't drive, so car travel isn't an everyday affair for me. I can make the short journey to church Sundays if we get a ride from the Kents or the Cooks. However, riding a cab to start a holiday makes me throw up, unless I swallow a liquid breakfast of milk only. I get to eat when we board the third train to Grandpa's. Meantime, in the back of this taxi, I clutch Darlene and wish Daddy would just shut up, so we could *get* to Union Station and continue on what seems to be the impossible journey.

As we exit the cab, Daddy makes a point of telling the driver why he is giving him a small tip.

"Oh, shush, Albert." Mom grabs one of the suitcases the driver has placed on the sidewalk and puts her spare hand in my right.

Daddy picks up his duffel bag, and the three of us march into Union Station.

Inside the Great Hall, I soak in the hushed din of voices gliding off the tiled vault ceiling and the various waiting rooms and hallways of this station, which took over a dozen years to build until the CNR and CPR cooperated. With the blessing of His Royal Highness, Edward, the Prince of Wales, Union Station (still not quite completed) opened August 6, 1927. After an 11-minute ceremony, the first ticket went to the Prince, a $71.20 ride to Alberta,[2] not bad for the first collection, but not as good as it gets for Mommy and me. As Daddy's immediate family, we receive free train rides.

A chime now blares, calling all the faithful travellers to listen.

"Train No. 136 for West Toronto, Hamilton, Brantford, Grimsby, St. Catharines, and Niagara Falls is now boarding on Platform 4."

The announcer's voice sooths my mind like the drone of the *Kyrie Eleison* at Mass. I stand still on the herringbone-patterned marble floors and gaze up at the names of Canadian cities carved high on the north and south walls. These names are testimonials to CNR and CPR stops, and looking at

---

[2] *A History of Union Station, City of Toronto Archives*, City of Toronto, 1998-2004.

their inscription on the stoned walls [3] leaves me standing with my mouth open. Union Station is like a church.

"Sharon, come on." Mom's voice is like the devil come to church, although the real devil is more likely Daddy, up ahead several feet and turning impatiently back to the dawdlers in his group.

We follow him, past the baggage check, which he ignores, and make our way over to the information counter where he confirms the departure platform number. Mom sets down the big suitcase, and I lift Darlene and let her look around.

Then we are speeding down the corridor ramp connecting the main concourse with the departure waiting area. A long line-up winds around from the second track. Daddy straightens up his short stature, puts a stern look on his face, and creates a gap between a mother and her five children, while my mother murmurs an "excuse me." I follow like the little lamb, not to slaughter, but to the fold of the railway station. Daddy leads us over to Platform 9, to the front of the non-existent line-up, just behind the roped-off gate. I'm right with him when he again looks at his watch. I can't wait to get on the train.

"It's 9 a.m.; the train doesn't leave until 10.10 a.m." Daddy nods his head.

That seems like a long time to an eight-year-old, so I start squirming.

"Sharon, do you have to go to the washroom?" Mom asks. She doesn't wait for my answer, but turns to Daddy. "You can watch the bags." Then she leads me, still clutching Darlene and my purse, to the Ladies near the corridor to the concourse—the same washroom where she cleaned me up last year after I got sick in the taxi. At least the vomit blended in with the red and black floral-on-yellow design of the new dress she had just sewn for me.

---

[3] Ibid. The specifics, not the author's church-like reference, of Union Station. From *A History of Union Station*, City of Toronto Archives, City of Toronto, 1998-2004.

We return to the platform gate and find Daddy waving around an envelope in his right hand and staring down at his watch on the other. He paces back and forth, his territory somewhat limited because there are now actually people lined up behind us.

"9.10 a.m.," he says. "They should be letting us on by now. Typical CNR."

Mom grits her teeth, and I look at Daddy's duffel bag and the big suitcase Mom and I share. Someone behind me coughs, and Mom nudges me.

"It won't be long now, Sharon," she says. "When we get on the train, we can get out your colouring book. Here, sit down on the suitcase."

I sit down, place Darlene on my lap, and start swinging my right foot back and forth.

A man wearing a black uniform trimmed in gold with a matching box-shaped cap appears as if he had beamed down from heaven.

"Have your train tickets ready because we're boarding in five minutes," he says.

Daddy removes our train passes from the envelope. His free ride and Mom's are for life and my children's pass lets me ride the rails until I turn 19, too far in the future for a kid who can't wait to get on the train *now*. Finally, the official opens the rope, and I expect Daddy to charge in like a bad bull, but he smiles, waves the passes at the official, then solemnly leads the procession up the stairs to the altar above.

The platform is big and black with the green coaches spread long like a silent hulk down the tracks. Another official wearing the standard black and gold CNR uniform stands at the bottom of the metal staircase leading into one of the coaches.

"Board here for Guelph," he says, and checks our passes dangling from Daddy's hand. "Uh huh," he says and grabs the suitcase and duffel bag, lifting them up onto the narrow wedge between train coaches. "Watch your step, little girl," and he takes my hand until I stand on the square footstool at the bottom of the stairs.

Daddy is already ahead of me and reaches down for my hand. I grab his hand and hang on tight as I take baby steps up. The metal stairs sound like tin beneath my feet. Then we need an usher because Daddy is prancing up and down the aisles, checking out the seats, all the same pale powdery green with a plastic bib draped over the top of their backsides.

"This one will do." Daddy points to one on the right, a few rows in from the corridor. He flips the back, and now two sets of seats face each other.

I sit next to the window and place Darlene on my lap. Mother plunks herself down beside me and straightens the hem of her dress. After Daddy places the big suitcase on the seat opposite Mommy and lifts the duffel bag onto the overhead rack, he sits down facing me.

"You're going to ride backwards, Daddy?" I ask.

"Yes," he says, but he seems distracted and keeps looking up at the overhead rack. Then he stands up and gives the duffel bag a shove, but it is already up against the wall.

"These racks are too small," he says. "Typical CNR."

"Shush, Albert," Mom says. "Sharon, would you like your colouring book and crayons?" She stands up and leans over the big suitcase.

"I'm hungry," I say.

Mom frowns. "You have to wait until we get on the train at Palmerston." She switches to a smile. "How about a drink of water?"

My stomach rumbles, but I nod. It will have to do.

"All aboard." The trainman's voice drifts in from the corridor ahead, and then the corridor door slams shut. Looking up, I lean over, nearly falling onto Mom when something jerks under my feet, below the floor.

"Be careful, Sharon," Mom says. "Sit in your seat."

But the jarring underfoot has added a roll. When I look out the window, the train two tracks over seems to be going backwards. Then the whistle toots, and we pick up a little speed. I smile and hold my breath. My church has switched to the ride of my life. I'm ready to roller-coast along to wherever it takes me.

The sun glares through the window making me blink. Daddy is already yanking down the window shade, but he's pulled it too far. I get brave and move it up a few inches.

"I want to see out, Daddy." I gaze at him. He smiles and pulls the blind up some more. I smile back and stare out the window.

Instead of wide green countryside, city streets whiz by below us. We are thumping across a bridge. The west end of Toronto's industrial area flashes by—dirty factory buildings spewing out smoke, then small deserted side streets fanning out from some nebulous beginnings underneath us, old tiny corner stores waiting for the children to come in and buy the five-cent ice cream cones or packets of Juicy-Fruit gum. Then we hit some of the city's dregs—thin, weathered houses cramped side by side, and endless streams of laundry hanging and blowing in the backyards. The children playing in the yards seem like rabbits darting around; I will them with my eyes to go to the corner stores. By then we are off the bridge. I get my country, if you can call a field of dandelions, daisies, and tall crab grass—country. Then that's gone, and it is more houses and laundry, but now the children in the backyard are waving. I wave back, not realizing that they probably can't see me clearly through the glass window.

"Have your train tickets ready," a now familiar male voice says.

The trainman who checked our tickets and passes in the station is standing by our seats. Daddy hauls out our passes.

"Are we running on time?" he asks.

"Yes, sir," the trainman replies. He glances at our passes, hands them back to Daddy, punches a couple of what looks like transfers and slides them in the window shade. "Change at Guelph and Palmerston." He winks at me.

As he moves to the next seat, Daddy looks at him as if he had failed kindergarten.

"Typical CNR," he mutters.

I spend the rest of this train ride staring out the window, waiting to leave Toronto as we stop at Parkdale, West Toronto, and Weston. Finally, we're out of the city, and the train charges forward, barrelling and bumping along the tracks. This time we pass real fields with cows, wheat stooks, corn stalks, and horses bobbing by.

Somewhere between the corn and wheat fields, Daddy excuses himself to go to the smoking coach to partake of his nemesis. He doesn't make any "typical CNR" comment, although he would be right. Light years away from municipal policing of smokers, in the 1950s and early 1960s, trains came equipped with separate smoking coaches. The rest were easy breathing zones, although if you opened a window, you inhaled the engine steam.

No steam engines on this train to Guelph—it rolled along pulled by one of the new whippersnappers called a diesel locomotive. But I get my steam engine at Guelph. We're waiting outside on the Guelph platform for our train to Palmerston. I hear a distant whoo-oo, whoo-oo that steadily grows louder and then chug-chug- whoo-oo as another train rounds the corner. I put Darlene to my left ear and my right hand over my right ear, purse dangling from my right arm. Thick charcoal smoke whirls up behind the chimney top of the massive black engine charging into the station. The smoke resembles a cloud of dark incense, but smells like soot mixed with tar. This engine leads like a big God with a stern round face who commands respect and suddenly I feel back in church. When this God comes to a halt, its mixed bag of followers—mail cars, baggage cars and passenger cars—stop. I remove my hand and doll from my ears. Daddy leads the way towards the train; Mom grabs my arm, and we follow him inside. We sit on powder blue seats that are stiff like old world furniture. As the train starts up, I glance across the aisle out the window on the other side. A wad of thick smoke billows up. Turning to my window, I look out and down. Right up against the tracks is a paved road and on its far side nestle rows of frame houses, with front yards of flowers and green grass. I rush to the other side for a better look out the window. More house fronts bob up in the smoke. The road also runs beside the railway tracks. The train is travelling down the middle of a street in the city of Guelph. So will its descendant in the twenty-first century.

We get off at Palmerston. The train taking us to Mildmay sits still on another track. I look at the black engine attached to one coach, an elegant sleeper car, Daddy tells me as we climb aboard. The inside smells of sturdy Victorian—polished dark wood walls with trim on the top of the seats. These seats don't swing around and with all that wood their backs can't slide to either side.

"At night when you want to sleep, the backs go down," Daddy says, but doesn't demonstrate. He points up to the overhead curved wood storage area. "That's the upper berth. That's for sleeping, too."

The seats already face each other, so we can just sit down. I take my usual spot by the window. The seat is stiff and its woolly material tickles my bare legs. Daddy leans over and pushes up one of the tall narrow windows.

Maybe it's the relaxed mood created by sitting in a sleeper car or maybe it's because this train isn't going anywhere for half an hour, but Mom hauls out the Spam sandwiches she made with white bread and butter, and hands me one wrapped in wax paper. I eat it fast and don't get sick. After hours of fasting, it tastes delicious. Then I notice that except for two other collections of passengers scattered throughout the one coach, this train is truly a sleeper.

Daddy, Mommy and I did more than just ride the rails to Mildmay and Lucknow. We also travelled the high waters to the United States.

***

One hot summer day in 1954, when the heat is singeing my eyelashes and the sweat is pouring down the front and back of my sleeveless blouse, Mom comes up with her plan to get us out of Toronto.

"We're going to Detroit to visit your Aunt Minnie and Uncle Terry," she says.

Going to Detroit to visit this aunt and uncle and my five cousins takes us, train included, across the Detroit River. The train doesn't chug through the water; it sails, sort of, on a paddle-wheeled steamer called the *Landsdowne*.

Getting railway passengers across the Detroit River went through several changes. From 1854 to the mid-1860s, passengers had to get off the trains at the Windsor, Ontario Station, board a ferry across the Detroit River, then at Detroit switch to the American railroad system because the Canadian railway company, then the Great Western Railway (GWR), pulled what Daddy would call a "typical CNR." The Canadian railway tracks were built to an off-standard gauge of 5'6" and didn't match their American counterpart. Finally, GWR built a third rail to get the US trains rolling on its tracks. That meant a huge change in ferry setup, as now the whole passenger train boarded the boat.

Enter the *Landsdowne* in 1891,[4] at 312 feet, the longest ferry on the Great Lakes. That summer of 1954, Mom, Daddy and I were fortunate to take one of its last runs because in September 1955 or 1956,[5] depending on your source, the CNR pulled the plug on passenger railway/ferry service. Once again passengers had to disembark from a train at Windsor and board an American train at Detroit. This time a bus carried them through the Detroit-Windsor tunnel.

But to a five-year-old, the river run is a big sea adventure filled with rollicking train coaches and the screech of metal wheels on steel rails as the train jerks and jolts onto the long open freighter. Instead of the train whistle, we get the foghorn call of the boat and the floor seems to zig and zag. I hang onto the seat, but I also look out the window. The train appears to be moving on water, as if its wheels are kicking through the river.

"Do you want to have a look from the back?" Daddy asks.

I nod and look at Mom, expecting a "no," from her. "My stomach feels okay."

---

[4] Oxford, William. *The Ferry Steamers: The Story of the Detroit-Windsor Ferry Boats*. Erin, ON: Boston Mills Press, 1992.

[5] *The Landsdowne* was turned into a floating restaurant on the Detroit side of the river.

She grabs my hand; we stand up and follow Daddy who is already up and in the aisle. We head to the back of the train and I gasp. The doorway is wide open and an expansion gate blocks our exit out onto the boat. On the other side of the gate, the top of the boat sits level with the tracks, and beyond is the city of Windsor, fast disappearing as the boat-train sloshes and kicks its way through the dark green Detroit River. As the waves shoot up and the train rocks, my head and heart fill with wonder, but my stomach stays calm. Years later, when my son and I first board my friend's sailboat, we will sit in it as it bobs, anchored to the dock in Lake Simcoe, and my friend will wait while I eat a bunch of grapes to see if I get sick when we set sail. I don't. My boat-train experience on the Detroit River will have a lasting effect.

***

During another summer adventure, Mommy, Daddy and I are on our way to Rochester, New York. This time we're travelling CPR because their route is direct and the family passes extend to CPR. The cars seem sparse, drab and green inside, with high-backed seats covered in burgundy plastic. But I'm not paying too much attention to inert details because on this trip my Daddy runs into one of his railway buddies, and I make a new friend.

We're on our way home, and I'm nodding off to the railway beat, my nine-year-old body tired of playing with Darlene the doll and reading *The Bobbsey Twins*. As usual, Daddy has a case of the wanders, and Mom stares out the window.

"Julia, I saw Roger in the parlour car." Daddy's voice drifts into my sleep. I miss the next few words, until "and his daughter, Barbara, is with him. She's about Sharon's age."

I sit up and see Daddy nodding at me.

"Huh?" I ask.

"Would you like to come and meet Barbara?" Daddy says. "Someone to play with, Sharon."

I look at Mom.

"Sure, go, but be back before we get near Toronto," Mom says.

"Do you want to come, too?" Daddy looks over at her.

"No. Someone has to stay here with the suitcases and I think I'll just rest for a bit."

I stand up before they can change their minds. Daddy takes my hand and leads me through the coach; he opens the door and we rock on the tiny platform joining the coaches and roll into the next coach and the next, until we hit the parlour car. The single high-backed seats with wings are placed living-room style in small circles, with people sitting in them. Some hold and wrap the newspaper in front of them, as if to absorb the copy in some semblance of privacy, while others lean forward and chat. Barbara and her dad fit the latter group, although Barbara is standing and jiggling beside her dad's chair.

She is something like The Bully, without the mean streak, but she has that leadership quality that I find nebulous in myself. She is also like me, an only child. I am drawn to her like fire to gasoline, and we hit it off as fast friends, although I don't suddenly turn talkative. I discover she lives five blocks from me, on the same street as my piano teacher, but on the other side of O'Connor. When this trip is over, we continue our friendship all the way into an adventure in the Don Valley.

Daddy, Mommy and I continued riding the rails. Despite his curmudgeonly attitude, I think he enjoyed the rides. It was his way of showing something important in his life to me. He also gave me the legacy of becoming a railway brat, something I can't seem to kick decades later. I also inherited his penchant for an obsession with time. But back then, time was not yet that essential to me. However, train travel always leading to a destination was. For us, destination usually meant family. But sometimes it was new adventures. Despite my scaredy-cat outlook, I looked forward to what happened after we stepped off the train.

5: Destination Stateside

Certainly, travel is more than the seeing of sights; it is a change that goes on, deep and permanent, in the ideas of living.
— **Miriam Beard,** Detroit, Michigan

I stand and stare around the small living room of Uncle Terry's and Aunt Minnie's Project home. After the boat-train trip across the Detroit River, I now feel lost, closed in and overwhelmed. The scene could pass for surreal in a box—bright lights glaring on every square inch and curtains fluttering in the background with teen boys and girls coming in and out from behind the curtains. I clutch Mom's hand and seem to shrink into the floor of this tiny house.

The curtains are the doors to three bedrooms fanning off this main room. One room for the parents, one for the two boys, Gordon and Bob, and one for the three girls, Cheryl, Brenda, and Laurie. I don't know where Mom, Daddy, and I will sleep. The living room?

For now I stick to Laurie, at 11, closest to my five and a half years.

It's around 9 p.m., late for me to be jaunting around in a strange city. I hold tight to Laurie's hand as we walk to a store to buy penny candy. Streetlights spring overhead from the darkness. Horns honk as drivers scoot along the road, their beams darting through nightfall. A breeze wafts around us. My head spins up, down, and around. I have stepped outside the surreal box into a surreal world, and it seems both unnatural and awesome.

Laurie and I spend our days playing with dolls. I play with a black baby doll, probably Laurie's.

On my next visit to Detroit, five years later, the trains no longer sit on the deck of the boats and sail across the Detroit River. No matter. Mom takes me on a mini-cruise from Detroit to Boblo Island. It is an evening tour. I find it strange that we are actually returning to Canada as Boblo is located on the Canadian side of the river. Daddy remains behind to drink with Uncle Terry.

The air smells like sweet Mississippi River, and the music aboard ship gets inside my soul—the high melodic trumpets mingling with the deep bold sax. The adult couples drift onto the floor and begin to dance. I have to get up and move. I envision a tall handsome man steering me around as I swoon to the music. But I am only 10 and with my Mom.

"Mom, let's dance." I say.

She just looks at me as if I said her slip was showing.

"Please, Mommy."

"Okay." She takes my arms and leads me out onto the dance floor. It is smooth gliding, and the music soothes right into my heart. I imagine it is really a handsome young man I am with. Only a few seconds of "I must look silly dancing with my Mom" flit through my head. At least, we're not in skates, with me trying to stay up as Mom steers me around the backyard skating rink.

On another day, Aunt Minnie, Mom, and I are returning from shopping at Hudson's Department Store on Woodward Avenue. We ride in the front of the bus, and the blacks, or "niggers" as they are called then, ride in the back.

The bus stops and starts. I remember it is hot and humid outside and that black and white people drink from separate fountains in Woodward's and Hudson's Department stores. This separation of the blacks and whites strikes me as odd. There is a black fellow from Jamaica in my class at Holy Cross Grade School and he isn't separated from the rest of us. So why here? Another visit to Detroit in my late teens will show me why.

6: Destination—Rural One

A child needs a grandparent, anybody's grandparent, to grow a little more securely into an unfamiliar world.

—Charles and Ann Morse

I'm hiding in the dining room of my Grandfather's farmhouse. While peeking through the window curtain, I keep quiet because what's happening outside is none of my six-year-old business.

Grandpa's and Grandma's dining room resonates with mustiness and an overall sense of black doom. Dark leather chairs sit tight against the bare table. In the corner stands the china cabinet, asleep to the world for years. But early 19th century décor and dust don't interest me. My eyes focus outside the window, past the large veranda, past the weeds, past the gravel driveway curving in from the nearby dirt road, and right under the tree where the driveway turns towards the barn.

Grandpa Charlie and a strange man stand talking under this tree. Behind them rests a trailer, back open, awaiting its passenger. But Grandpa isn't going for a ride. The traveller is the chestnut brown horse nosing the ground in front of the two men. The horse is old and obsolete, and his replacement, a huge Massey-Ferguson tractor, hides beyond my sight—at least, I guess it is parked by the barn, because I've seen this monster there before, and it terrifies me.

Although never having ridden, petted, fed or talked to this horse, I am drawn to him. *My Friend, Flicka* and *Fury*, both TV shows about a boy and his horse, enter my imagination and spawn side stories. I, who once found sitting atop a pony rough and dangerous, daydream about riding the winds on the back of this brown horse, its black mane flying behind. This horse will never giddy-up anywhere again. As the man puts a rope around its neck and leads it onto the trailer, I can't help shedding a tear, silent of course. If Grandpa Charlie sees me crying the blues over an old horse, he will frown.

Grandpa Charlie's stern silent look gives no clue to the real Grandpa. He stands tall, thin and proud, a fitting specimen of his German ancestry. He went bald early, except for sprigs of dark hair, which later turned white, on each side. He usually parks his hands together behind him or in his back overall pockets, unless I am around. What is it with grandfathers and granddaughters? Grandpa treats his children with discipline and an air of authority. But once the new grandchild appeared—especially the only child of one of his daughters—his attitude sharp-turned towards his heart. You would never guess that from the photos of my first time at Grandfather's farm near Mildmay, Ontario. Grandpa appears to be hanging on for dear life to me, and Grandma has a "for goodness sake, Charlie she's only a baby" look on her face.

Grandpa and Grandpa's farm is the first stop for Mommy, Daddy and me on our annual summer pilgrimage by train. Despite regular rural passenger service, our train doesn't go as far as the end of my grandparents' laneway. Instead it chugs into the train station, a relic from the Grand Trunk Railway days, located on the edge of town.

When the sleeper coach train pulls into the Mildmay station, we don't bother to go inside. Uncle Theodore, one of Mom's younger brothers is waiting outside by his old black Packard. He grabs the rear door, opening it from front to back. Mom and I climb in; Daddy sits upfront with Uncle Theodore. He tries to make conversation, but is hit by my uncle's shy vow of silence. Mom chirps in.

We turn onto Highway 9, which becomes Elora Street for the main drag of this farming community town. This street appears swathed in sand, humidity and sunlight, the former reflecting on the area's large chunks of sand and gravel. Uncle Theodore stops at the feed co-op and Bieman's Creamery. Inside the car, the still heat engulfs us, and my nose stuffs up. The beige seat covered in fake velvet pricks my bare legs no matter how I try to sit. I poke my head outside the window, trying to see if Uncle Theodore is finally returning. Mom's and Daddy's voices are like the drone of flies. This city child opens her mouth and yawns.

**

My memories of Grandpa and Grandma's farm didn't start until I was about six. Although I always remembered that the farm stood at a corner two miles outside of Mildmay, years later I will go on a merry hunt to find its actual legal location—a necessary prerequisite to uncovering the farm's history after Grandpa's ownership.

Grandpa Charlie was a man of property. When his father died in 1912, Grandpa found himself temporarily, part owner of a 20-acre farm outside Mildmay in the Township of Carrick along with his mother and his 10 siblings. While she could live there the rest of her life, my great grandmother was so ticked off that her husband didn't will her full ownership, she partnered with one daughter to buy another house in town.

Grandpa picked up the property pace. The next farm property bought contained the yellow brick house where my mother and her seven siblings (including one stillborn between her and Uncle Theodore's birth) were born between 1903 and 1919. This gang had no problem travelling to the one-room school—it stood (and still does, but later became a private summer home) down the hill from the driveway of the farmhouse. Although Grandma and Grandpa could see the school from the farmhouse window or the field, that didn't stop this gang of siblings, particularly my godfather, from dawdling to and from classes. Anything to delay doing the chores.

During the Depression my grandfather did the unthinkable—bought another farm, a mile and a quarter down Concession Six for $8,750. But farmers purchased for the land—the house came "as is."

When Mommy, Daddy, and I visit this second farm with its red brick house, I feel as if I have entered Otherland, a place filled with open spaces outside, and varying textures of light and darkness inside. To reach the light, I have to climb up the dark enclosed wooden stairway, past the door at the bottom to Uncle Theodore's bedroom (which has another door leading to the tiny living room), and push open the door at the top of the stairs. There, the brightness overwhelms me. I run up and down the halls, poking my head into each room.

"This room is Aunt Gretchen's," I mutter. "Here's where my godfather slept when he still lived at home." I like this room, sitting front and centre in the sunlight. However, Mom and I usually sleep across the hall, or the middle-of-the-corridor bedroom or the big master bedroom at the back of the hall. Daddy gets whatever is left.

The sunniest side of the master bedroom holds the double bed. I open the closet door beside the bed and am nearly blinded by the sunlight streaming in from the bare window onto the bare walls and the floor containing a pile of odds and ends, probably long forgotten by Grandma and Grandpa. I cover my eyes and hurry back into the main room, charging across to the opposite side, opening yet another door onto a narrow balcony. I run down the back stairway to the back kitchen and head out the side door. I grab one of the feral barn kittens to play with and take it onto the cool porch outside the main kitchen.

Usually I clomp down the enclosed stairwell and open the door to the hub of the house, the big kitchen. Colour it middle bright, depending on the time of day and how many family members are congregating there. I sit on the couch under the window by the porch while Mom and Aunt Gretchen dance their cooking territorial rights by the big black wood stove.

They are a pair, those sisters. Gretchen, the elder, barely scraping 4 ft. 11, stocky in her sensible black oxfords and a floral or striped housedress drooping to mid-calf. She makes Mom appear elegant at 5 ft. 1 in her housefrau dress. Gretchen cracks open eggs into a large bowl, picks up a fork, and begins whipping. Her chin-length hair, straight from its left side part, bobs and shakes in thin shards to the beat of her hand. Meantime, Mom minds the potatoes. Their dual act extends beyond preparing the day's dinner. Mother plays Hastings to Gretchen's Hercule Poirot, although the subject isn't exactly murder. To hear Gretchen drone about the evils of fluoridation, you can be forgiven if you think you should call the police.

"It's the Communists who are to blame, Julia," she says. She whips the eggs faster as if to accentuate her point. She stops, not to catch her breath, but to drop her bomb. "It gives you cancer." She grins at Mom, as if daring her to argue.

Mom's only answer comes in the chop-chop of the knife, first through the potatoes, then the onion. I flee upstairs and cower in the sunny closet off the master bedroom or the dark closet down the hall. Or I run outside and cuddle one of the barn cats. Scarredy-cat Sharon prefers diseased cats to the venom spewing from Gretchen's mouth.

One late afternoon Gretchen takes on Grandpa; I don't remember what they argue about, but let's just say that they have words. I cower in the kitchen corner up front by the pantry doorway, perhaps seeing it as a place to hide if things get too rough for little eyes and ears. The two face off from their various positions in the farm kitchen, Grandfather sitting on the couch under the window, Gretchen banging at a pot on the stove. Their voices rise as if in pre-arranged disharmony.

"No, that's not right. They'll take over, and we will all die." Gretchen's grin has now changed to a snarl. Her hair hangs down like some cave-era warrior and she clutches the pot handle, as if ready to heave its contents across the kitchen.

"Now, that's enough, Gretchen," Grandfather says in his wheezy voice. He stands up, stretching his thin form up tall, pulling on the suspenders of his black trousers. His hooked nose can't quite hide his twisted mouth or the thin translucent teeth. I back into the pantry.

Of course, I don't remember their exact words, but remember the tone, the underlying battle of father and daughter. I peek out, waiting for Grandfather to rush towards the stove and strike Gretchen. Would she have actually hurled the pot of boiling water at him? However, this and other arguments never escalate to physical violence. Just words inflicted on each other.

Sometimes Daddy and Grandpa Charlie sit on the couch under the front window and try to talk. But they have little in common except Mom and me, so Daddy usually acts like the lost soul, pacing around outside on the farm, his hands in his right pocket jingling the keys inside. Sometimes I watch him from the window; sometimes I walk outside onto the veranda. He stops his wandering and looks over at me. I smile. He nods back. Sometimes I join him. Sometimes I don't, so he continues, his walk now more like a stroll.

However, Grandpa and I have our moments of clicking together across the generations. Grandpa wants to show the farm to city kid me.

We are in the barn, and the pungent smells of cows, chickens and hay stifle my nostrils. Hay is stacked to the ceiling. Years later, my godfather will tell me that when the grain was ripe in the fields he, Uncle Theodore, Uncle Thomas, and Grandpa used to bind it and put it into sheaves. They tied a border around them and stacked them up in five to six sheaves outside to dry in the sun before the rain came.

But Grandpa is focused on the chickens. "Come on Sharon, let's go collect some eggs." He takes my hand.

Taking slow steps through the hay sprawled on the wooden floor, I wonder if my running shoes will ever get clean. When Grandpa opens a door to the left, clusters of hens spring into the air. I jump back at the feathers flying and the scolding at our interruption. I look around for the rooster, but he's probably taking a long nap to give him energy to stand up at dawn and wake up the farm. My feet sink into deep layers of hay.

"They won't hurt," Grandpa says. "See, these ones over here, they're the laying hens. Hold the basket, and we'll go check them for eggs."

I clutch the basket as if it's my lifeline. I'm not going to hurt you chickens I silently tell them, but they still seem lively, carrying on their clucking conversations. Grandpa gently slips his hand under first one chicken, then the other, and it's like magic. He holds a couple of eggs in his hand and places them in my basket. Funny, I consider it is now "my basket." Keeper of the eggs, but never grabber of the eggs.

"Do you want to collect some eggs?" Grandpa asks. I stand there, gripping the basket.

Two summers later, when I am eight, I show no qualms about marching into the henhouse in the barn with the 13-year-old hired hand. I don't want to show this red-haired guy with freckles that I'm chicken. I help collect eggs and even manage to wander through the main area of the barn. The air is filled with the smell of sweet pungent hay, the sweaty old-underwear tang of the cows in the stable below. Then I hear a tinkle of water hitting the floor. I peek beyond the haystacks and see Grandpa peeing. Embarrassed, I turn quickly away. This farm doesn't have a modern bathroom.

Later, inside the farmhouse kitchen, Grandpa and I engage in the unholy battle of shooting hard flat pellets across the table. We're playing Crokinole to win, and I'm at a disadvantage with my tiny kid fingers.

"Use your thumb and middle finger like this," Grandpa says. He stares down the black pellet located in circle number five on his side of the octagonal board. He frowns in concentration, then joins his thumb and middle finger, thumb underneath, finger above and, somehow, flicks them together, sending the pellet bouncing high and mighty, knocking off first one, then two of my timid white pellets. I squint and wonder how to move either of my remaining two pellets on the board.

I am too short to shoot sitting down, so I stand up. I do the thumb-finger thing and stare at the pellet. *Move*, my eyes seem to say. Then I take a deep breath and flick. But it is finger action only. The pellet sits still like a plane with no fuel.

With the next try, fingers and pellet connect, and the pellet takes off, high like a two-seater airplane performing stunts, but the only stunt this airborne pellet does is hit the edge of the table and land in Grandpa's lap.

It will take considerable time for me to learn and relearn to shoot to score, and not only playing Crokinole. Life is filled with games of ups and downs and knowing when, where and how to fly, and land with feet on the ground. Back then, I had both Grandpa and Daddy to show me the ropes, to be around when I took a fall. Being a kid, I thought they would both be there forever. I didn't realize it could be just for a while and I could be the only player on the Crokinole board. It doesn't matter if you choose black or white pellets, because nothing *is* black or white only—often life's challenges come in shades of grey, or worse, black turns white and white turns black, and you sometimes end up shooting crap and having it boomerang at you.

Not all our trips to Grandpa and Grandma's farm were during the summer. We stayed for a few days and nights in late November 1957 when Grandma died. I was never close to her. She came across as a vague person—not all there, but she did have dementia and, after she fell and broke her hip, she lived in her bed.

When I think of Grandma dying, I think of the stuffy, moth-smelling funeral home in Mildmay. Religious rituals fascinate me, so when I discover that violet is the colour of sorrow, I play it for all its worth.

"Mama is wearing a purple dress; the flowers are purple, and look, my dress has purple in it, too. We're all ready for the funeral." I skip around the funeral parlour, and my godfather and godmother smile.

7: Destination—Rural Two

This isn't good or bad. It's just the way of things. Nothing stays the same.
—**Anonymous**, RealLivePreacher.com Weblog, January 03, 2004

"Come on Sharon; you can sit in the back between your Aunt Gretchen and me." Mom holds the car door open and points. I hide my displeasure in sniffles, squeeze in beside Aunt Gretchen, and hope she will keep her mouth closed. I don't want to referee her comments to my mother about bad water getting into our taps. So I look past Mommy out the window as farm after farm slides by.

This trip is no sleek train ride. Uncle Theodore always drives us to my godmother's farm in his black Packard. Daddy sits up front beside him. No matter what day we arrive at Grandpa's farm, we always leave on a Sunday afternoon after morning Mass. We load that Packard up with our suitcases and ourselves and travel the 30 miles on back roads from Grandpa's farm near Mildmay to my godmother's and Uncle Stanley's farmhouse on the 11th concession dirt road, southwest of Lucknow.

Visiting my godmother's farm seems almost halfway to staying at a resort villa—at least after Grandpa Charlie's farm with no central heating, no bathrooms and no running water. Like Grandpa's farm, my godmother's place has electricity, but it also has central heating—if you call an oil-burning stove in the kitchen with pipes throughout the house, central—and running water from a basement shower and two kitchen sinks with taps. The end of the kitchen, near the refrigerator, has Formica counter tops, dual steel sinks with one-spout taps, and a window overhead. Standing by the table, looking straight ahead, you can believe you are in the latest 1950s kitchen, albeit cramped, when five or six cousins no longer in a crib, my godmother and uncle, a farm hand, my parents, and I sit at the table eating roast beef and fried potatoes. It overwhelms a little girl who remains silent listening to the unfamiliar farming chatter at the table or from the radio on the nearby kitchen counter.

But swing around and look at the other end of the kitchen, and you enter an older world with the oil-burning stove, the summer kitchen doorway, and a flat utilitarian sink holding two taps with separate spouts. Towels hang on a rack to the right, and the always present bar of soap slops in the soap dish. This is the wash-up corner, the no-privacy hair rinsing/sponge bath area. Like Grandpa Charlie's farmhouse, this house contains no bathroom.

To do your business you step outside the rear door of the back kitchen and head down the path to the outhouse. Here, you contend with flies, stinks that you can't flush away, and in my case, one or two of my seven cousins banging on the outhouse door and teasing that they will come in. At night before retiring, Mom and Daddy take turns, winding down the trail to the outhouse. I usually go with Mom who carries toilet paper in her left hand. In her right hand she shines a flashlight in front, its light dancing in the dark, creating shadows on the periphery. When we return, she hands Daddy the flashlight.

The three of us sleep in the tiny living room across the narrow hall from the stairs to the second level. Mom and I are on a couch whose undercarriage rolls out into an instant trundle bed. Mom sleeps on the trundle, while I take the couch proper against the wall. Daddy sleeps on the other couch a couple of feet from Mom. If I wake up during the night I can hear him snore, loudly; it is comforting because he is here; Mommy is here, and so am I. First up in the morning is always Mommy, with me a close second. Daddy is the last to emerge for the day. Unlike his missteps with Grandpa, he does bond with Uncle Stanley. In the evenings, Daddy and Uncle Stanley sit around the kitchen table sharing a couple of bottles of beer, with Daddy smoking the inevitable cigarette. During the day, my uncle works the farm. I don't see too much of Daddy during the day, except at the midday meal when we all gather together around the kitchen table.

Instead, I play with my cousins, particularly the four oldest. It doesn't always sail smoothly, but I like to insert myself in my cousins' daily activities, despite sometimes feeling a bit shy. But it is never dull.

One day, Linda, Margaret, and I are holed up in front of the house, sitting in the family's green Packard, reading Archie comics, trying to keep cool. The car windows are wide open, but they don't let in even a smidgeon of a breeze, only the flies hot-tailing it on the scorching summer breeze. We start swatting at them with the comic books. Then we hear it.

Jimmie and my godmother are going at it like verbal wrestlers on the other side of the open house window. She's giving Jimmie holy hell, and he's not taking it.

"Jeepers, Jimmie, leave Jane alone." His mother's voice can still a fly, yet up the level of heat.

Linda, Margaret and I bury our noses in the comics, waiting for the rebuke.

"But Jane keeps butting in," Jimmie whines back. I imagine him facing his mom, hands on hips, lips snarling.

"Don't you sass me, Jimmie."

"I'm not."

"Jimmie, don't you speak to me like that."

And it continues—this battle for control. Eventually, Jimmie stomps out. From behind the comic book, I peek at him, hands in his pockets, glasses plunked on the bridge of his nose, and mouth closed into a pout. He has no use for us girls, and wanders off. I can hear him peeing behind the house. We girls continue swatting at the flies while trying to read.

I don't always hang around with the girls. Sometimes I need to play with someone closer to my age than Linda and Margaret. Jimmie and Karl as the oldest cousins are it. Once I get over that they are boys, we manage just fine.

As the sun slides down in the evening, Jimmie and Karl decide to teach me how to chase the cows home. Jimmie stretches the barbed-wired fence wide so I can climb through without ripping my arms or shorts. I appreciate that because back home, while tearing after my friends, I tried vaulting a fence, and the backside of my shorts stuck and ripped.

Once through the barbed wire, I stare at big beasts with mottled black and white skin and bodies remaining stationary, except at either end—the tails sliding back and forth keep me mesmerized. How can they chew the weeds and grass bits so matter-of-factly while their eyes seem to dig deep into my head? They must know how frightened I feel.

"They won't hurt you," Jimmie says. "Just don't run at them and startle them. Come on." He strolls forward, as if he has no concerns, and Karl follows.

I don't want my cousins finding out that I'm a scaredy-cat, so I follow, picking my way through mostly unseen black deposits scattered throughout the pasture. The cows become benign pets that we must set on the right track. We chase the herd from one field to another. Karl opens the gate, and the cows come home, not quite roller-skating, but close, because they suddenly surge in the gateway and settle down for the night in the pasture by the barn.

During the day, Jimmie, Karl, and I play in our own private sand pile behind the shed, off the path that winds from the house past my godmother's fenced-in vegetable garden. Away from parents' prying eyes, we create roads and highways and, with cries of "broom, broom," push toy cars, trucks and tractors along the super sand highway.

This idyllic life on the farm will soon crash, and like my own family circle, it will be from illness and concern for the father. In the year of Our Lord, 1958, Uncle Stanley was helping dig the grave for a recently deceased friend and church member. It was the middle of February, freezing, with snow piled beyond any praying hands. The season of colds, flu and other deadly diseases had managed to dig through the winter's debris and grab onto anyone it could. Three weeks after his graveyard shift, Uncle Stanley was rushed to the hospital in London, Ontario. Diagnosis? Meningitis. There is really no proof Uncle Stanley contracted the disease from being out in the cold digging a grave, but in later years I would often wonder about that.

Of course, he died—a few days later in an impersonal hospital.

"No, Sharon you can't go," Mom says when I ask about his funeral. She mentions something about me getting sick after attending Grandma's funeral. My mother, the worrywart, might even have worried that I would get meningitis. So, Daddy has to stay home, too.

I don't feel right about missing Uncle Stanley's funeral. I think it has something to do with my seven cousins, all under 10 years, who are now fatherless. I feel sad and imagine baby Harry lying in his crib all alone, crying for a daddy who never comes. At least I still *have* my daddy around.

So, then it was just my godmother and those seven kids left to fend for themselves and the farm. But she never considered her family as poor. They had beef and dairy cattle, pigs and chickens. There was also that huge vegetable garden with its wrap-around wooden fence down the path from the house—a garden filled with carrots, beans, beets, corn, cucumbers, onions, tomatoes, and rhubarb. Nearby grew a large gooseberry patch. During my summer visits, I used to help Linda and Margaret pick berries, although I didn't find them sweet enough to eat raw. My godmother canned some of the vegetables and fruit. From all this (and a few items such as bread bought in town), she fed her family two big meals a day, never sandwiches, but there were always leftovers. She sewed Linda and Margaret dresses, which were passed along to Cheryl and Jane. When Cheryl balked at the hand-me-downs, she drove the four girls into town and bought them identical dresses. This younger sister of my mom had no problem receiving help with the farm work—the crops and the daily chores—first from her cousin Sheila until Sheila married, then from some of the neighbouring farmers, including Joe Prince from down the road.

In the summers after Uncle Stanley's death, Mom, Daddy and I continued to visit. Aunt Minnie, Mom's other older sister, and her children often travelled from Detroit to Grandpa Charlie's farm and then on to my godmother's. Was it because Minnie missed her siblings and parents or did she miss Canada? Uncle Terry became a US citizen, but his wife held onto her Canadian citizenship as if it were the tie to her real home. She often spoke about returning to Canada for good. In the meantime, she did these cross-border jaunts to connect her US family with her Canadian. Often these trips coincided with when Mom, Daddy, and I were visiting.

Laurie, Aunt Minnie, Mom, and I are sitting around my godmother's kitchen table. Aunt Minnie has a twinkle in her eye and she is ready for mischief. Don't let this fuzzy grey-haired lady with the pink cheeks fool you. Give her a deck of cards, and she'll "kill" any seasoned gambler. Aunt Minnie is a game shark. She hauls out a pack of cards:

"Let's play Pinochle," she says.

We play one-deck Pinochle because only four of us play. I don't remember the intricacies of the game, only Aunt Minnie whipping the cards around and throwing them down when she has a trick to play (that is part of the game). I remember better the other card game because it required a special deck of cards. Flinch has 150 cards, each one bearing a number from one to 15. The goal is to be the first to eliminate your game pile of cards, dealt at the beginning, by placing them in centre piles numbered from one to 15. Top-of-the-pile cards are turned face up. Sounds simple? You are picking up hands of five as you play, and what you can't play gets added to your game pile. Flinch also has a "must play first" rule—if you have a card in hand with the same number as a top pile card, you must play the pile card first or another player can call you on it.

Minnie puts her own twist on the game. When she spies me putting down an 11 from my hand, and my game pile sports an 11 on top, she yells, "Flinch." Her Detroit-rural Ontario drawl then turns to a cackle as she holds up her five cards, their backs to me.

"Pick one," she says.

My face burns scarlet and I feel stupid when grabbing the card in the middle and adding it to the bottom of one of my game stacks; then missing a turn. While Laurie, Mom, and Aunt Minnie play their hands, I alternate from watching their moves, taking stock of the piles on the table, and glancing at my table and hand piles. I am determined to win.

Not with Aunt Minnie around, and no wonder. She is a smart cookie. Aunt Minnie and Flinch started life in the same year, 1905, so they were fated to become a winning duo.

However, it is another family scene that will stick forever in my heart, in technicolour.

That summer, my family's farm visit expands to Lake Huron with its deep blue waters. To reach the beach, we drive south on Highway 21, turn right onto a dirt road just south of Kingsbridge, drive a little way in, and leave the car at the top of a hill. As we traipse down the narrow trail, part soil and wood steps, I keep close to Mom, digging my right hand into her left. My eyes almost form an unwelcome bond with the ground while making sure my sneakered feet do not dwell near any plants—a bit difficult as a forest surrounds us. I am terrified of brushing against poison ivy and looking like Dorothy's older sister Marge two summers ago. Marge's face and arms suddenly sprouted triple acne rolling in pus. Rumour had it she was hiking in the Don Valley.

But this beach is by Lake Huron, and the trail is actually very short. We soon reach deep sifting sand. My feet sink in. Mom and my godmother spread out blankets. I plunk down on one, remove my runners, wiggle my toes in the sand, and stare at the blue sky, the blue-green water, and the sun shining on them. You could actually see the sky-lake borders, not like today where the whole picture is a dingy blur that can cause cancer.

"The water's quite shallow." Mom's voice almost startles me. "You won't have any trouble wading through it. You just have to wear your running shoes."

The water appears calm, I glance down at bare feet and the nearby running shoes.

"Rocks," Mom says.

When we wade into the lake, I am thankful for the sneakers. I look down through the shimmering water, clear and clean, with a bottom that is not soft sand but hard white rocks. They aren't flat walk-on-rocks but are abstract projections which require a combination of stomp and slosh to manoeuvre my way far enough in the water until I stand underarm deep. When I want sand, I remove my waterlogged runners, stroll barefoot along the beach with my cousins, and collect seashells, or watch my cousins' mother with her then new close friend, Joe Prince. Joe and my godmother are wading in the water, splashing it at each other and laughing. For some reason, I feel embarrassed and look away.

I will drift back to the picture and see, over and over again, that summer on the edge of Lake Huron. Mom, one of my cousins, and I are sitting where the lake water slaps onto the beach. We look like seals. Another cousin stands nearby, pointing down at the water. The four of us are wearing bathing caps. Nearby on the sand, my godmother, who has torn herself away from Joe, stands in a huddle with Brenda and Laurie, who are also visiting. We all appear in black and white, but the lines are clear, unlike today where the parameters of our lives seem to spread like viruses.

Were things easier and simpler when everything we were supposed to do or not do was spelled out in black and white? Living by this code didn't guarantee no one would get sick and die too soon. My family is testimony to that. But when someone died, there were ground rules—not that everyone in my family always followed them.

But over 60 years ago on that Lake Huron beach, it is only the sun, sand, and hunger that interferes with our energy. Mom, Daddy, and my godmother have brought along solutions for the latter—buns, wieners, hamburgers, tomatoes, lettuce, and marshmallows in coolers. Joe, Daddy, and the boys collect driftwood, pile it up on the beach, and light our makeshift stove for dinner. Hamburgers (dressed with tomato and lettuce) taste smoky and crisp. When the sun dips below Lake Huron, we huddle, with sweaters, towels, and blankets around our shoulders and toast marshmallows. Joe has made a quick dash up to the cars and turned on the headlights. They create an eerie beam through the trees, and although it seems to blend with the firelight, I still feel like we are on our own island. We bask in our joint family circle around the fire, its light shimmering across the lake like a tunnel that ends sharply in blackness. We are at peace, content.

For now.

8: City Travels with Mom

Look at all the buses now that want exact change, exact change. I figure if I give them exact change, they should take me exactly where I want to go.
—George Wallace

As Daddy was to riding the rails, Mom was to city transit. She was my guide as we trekked around on Toronto's buses, streetcars, and subway. At the time, I just didn't realize how much of a guide and how far it extended beyond travelling local transit.

From 1953, Mom sure had a lot of choice to get us around Toronto on buses and streetcars—there were over 650[6] PCCs (Presidents' Conference Committee) streetcars to journey through, 35 new routes, 23 suburban routes, not to mention the extensions to 20 existing routes.[7] Way too much to take a little girl around. Before we could possibly travel through half that list I would be past my mother's age of 39 at the time. Like comedian Jack Benny, she hung onto 39, year after year, and I believed her. After all, she was Mom.

Just for the record, in January 1, 1954, a month after I turned 5, the TTC (with "transportation" now shortened to "transport") took over all these routes and vehicles.[8]

---

[6] Kohler, Peter C. Toronto's Boomer PCCs, May 31, 2020. Online, 2006. [accessed August 19, 2020], http://transit.toronto.on.ca/streetcar/4507.shtml

[7] *Toronto Transportation Committee*, Wikipedia. Online. [accessed February 26, 2019], http://en.wikipedia.org/wiki/Toronto_Transportation_Commission

Then the subway came to town. Mom, Daddy, and I missed the opening run.

This new subway, Toronto's first, actually started its chugging along on March 30, 1954, 1,695 days after construction first began. The fare, one way, was 10 cents cash or three tokens or tickets for 25 cents. The route ran 4.6 miles (7.4 km) north to Eglinton from Union Station.[9]

Mom and I soon made up for missing that first run. It also gave us Langevins a deeper riding choice. But first we had to catch the bus near home.

The bus stop closest to 139 was around the corner on O'Connor Drive—that is, if you walked left, and the TTC hadn't moved its trademark red and white sign to the far side of the nearest intersection. If we saw the bus coming, we played transit roulette with the streetlights, the driver's whim to wait for us, and the alternative—making a hasty right turn and sprinting to the next bus stop. Once we boarded the bus, we continued with the rest of our travels. Long languid rides on streetcars out to Long Branch in Toronto's west end. Short hops on buses to shop on the Danforth. Streetcars jam-packed with sugar-fuelled kids and yawning parents returning from a day at the CNE. Or emerging from the subway on Bloor Street east of Yonge and doing the freezing stomp while waiting inside the makeshift wood shelter for the streetcar. All before the Bloor subway line would open in 1966, something I wouldn't be aware of until I actually boarded it. However, despite being only kindergarten age, I do remember some of the Yonge-Eglinton subway's building phase.

Mom and I emerge from Eaton's or Simpsons department stores at Queen and Yonge Streets into a deconstructive mess. I stare at Yonge Street, a confusing mixture of big boards—wooden and steel—with holes in-

---

[8] Filey, Mike. *The TTC Story: The First Seventy-five Years*, Toronto, Dundurn Press, 1996.

[9] Toronto's first subway line ran from Eglinton Station to Union Station

between. It is enough to make my legs wobble and hang on tight to Mom's hand. I don't want to fall in and I sure don't want to do the steel walkway across Yonge Street at Queen or anywhere on Yonge St., especially in winter with the snow, slosh, and mud at our feet, plus the cold winds whipping everywhere. At least we can get on the Queen Streetcar without walking the steel plank. Once the subway opens, the mess above ground disappears, and we are warm and dry on the subway trains. I can hang onto Mom's hand. Riding on the subway trains fills me more with wonder than fear, although I avoid looking out the windows as the train zips through dark tunnels. Mom sits beside me, and I still believe she will keep me safe.

"Mind the doors. The doors are closing." The voice fills the train. But it is only the invisible announcer telling people to get inside fast.

The subway doors swoosh shut, and the train rumbles out of the Bloor subway station. On this trip, we are headed for somewhere in the northern regions beyond Toronto, beyond the last subway station at Eglinton. Daddy is along, so it must be Sunday, and we are going to visit some of my parents' cronies. Suddenly, like magic, bright light appears outside the windows. Sunlight. The train is out of the dark tunnels, rocking on the surface. It feels like riding on a real train—until I look down at what we are sitting on. Red vinyl seats, which are not individual seats like those in railway trains, but low-backed seats holding two people. Some seats also face sideways. The aluminum outside of the trains is also red, although the term "Red Rocket" originated with the PCC streetcars.[10] But streetcars and buses get stuck behind cars and trucks. It is the subway that travels like a rocket.

At Eglinton, we climb the stairs, board a diesel bus to the City Limits loop at Yonge Street. and Yonge Boulevard, where we switch to a trolley bus. We also pay another fare as we have entered another riding zone. Zones and their accompanying fares won't be removed until 1973. As the trolley

---

[10] City of Toronto, Toronto Transit Commission. May 7, 2009. Online. [accessed August 19, 2020], http://www.ttc.ca/News/2009/May/Historic_TTC_PCC_Streetcar_back_on_track.jsp

bus starts up, I look out the window at Toronto's ravines, and it feels as if we are bustling through a fairy-tale Greenland.

Besides the actual journey, the stops in between juxtaposed Mom and I like salt and pepper. In my kid years, this pairing seemed to draw us closer, as if we were big and little sister. But salt and pepper are opposites, salt is a stabilizer and pepper spices up your life. Getting the two to gel—stable and spice—can yank your life worse than standing on the subway, hanging onto the pole as the train twists around a curve into the Queen Street subway station and the shopping kingdoms above.

The 1950s and early 1960s were the heydays of the big department stores—Simpsons and three Eaton's stores downtown. The latter stores originated with a small Toronto shop, which Timothy Eaton opened at Queen and Yonge Street in 1869, and replaced with the four-storey flagship Eaton's in 1883.[11] In 1930, The ritzy Eaton's College Street Store opened at College Street and Yonge Street.[12] Mom turned up her country nose at it and steered me towards its opposite, The Eaton's Annex, on Albert Street. Did Mom gravitate towards this store because its three storeys and basement sat on a downtown street carrying Daddy's name? Or was it the anticipation and joy of flipping through clothes and shoes piled on tables in the basement, and if you were lucky, find a bargain that you weren't embarrassed to wear?

More than the clothes, I remember the soft ice cream, the elevators, and the escalators.

"Hold onto the railing, Sharon," Mom says, as we stand at the top of an escalator.

I dig my hand into the railing, peek down, and hesitate before gingerly placing toes, then whole feet on the escalator floor. I expect the floor to

---

[11] *Eaton's*, Wikipedia, the free encyclopedia. Online. [accessed February 26, 2019], https://en.wikipedia.org/wiki/Eaton%27s

[12] *The Carlu*, Wikipedia, the free encyclopedia. Online. [accessed February 26, 2019], https://en.wikipedia.org/wiki/The_Carlu

change to steps, like those at the main Eaton's store, but it remains a series of slabs rudely jutting out. Riding up makes me feel as if I'm on a conveyor belt in a factory assembly line; riding down is akin to standing on a roller coaster without the safety bar across your front.

The elevators, off in their own hallway, are an earlier version of panoramic elevators, except the view is inside the shaft while you wait outside the glass door for the elevator's arrival. I close my eyes, hang on tight to Mommy's hand, and try not to think of freefalls.

But we arrive safely back in the basement or "subway" as Eaton's calls it. I deserve the hot dog and soft white ice cream whirled into a cone sold at a stand near the underground walk to the main Eaton's Store.

But never on a Saturday afternoon in August. Eaton's in the 1950s is closed Saturdays at 1.30 p.m. This harkens back to the founder, Timothy Eaton, closing the store at 2 p.m. Saturdays in July and August.[13] Today's constant shoppers would never go for this; however, they now can shop online 24/7.

During my shopping trips with Mom, I just want to absorb all the mid-1950s amenities. Both Simpsons and Eaton's pamper women and children. At one of the stores, we usually stop at the Ladies, then the waiting room next door. The room resembles a miniature hotel lobby with couches, pre-Lazy Boy recliners, writing tables and chairs. Mom and I sit at a couple of these tables. She hauls out some cards and writing paper; after handing me some of the latter she gets right down to the business of correspondence.

At first, I sit, look around and absorb the subdued atmosphere. Then I am transformed into a woman of business who must write letters, so I start to scribble. I have no idea what, probably rubbish.

Sometimes Mom takes me shopping Saturdays on the Danforth. It has everything from food to shoes with some messy bits along the way. Daddy doesn't come along. This is Mommy-and-me time. But first we have

---

[13] Macpherson, Mary-Etta. *Shopkeepers to a Nation.* Toronto, McClelland and Stewart Ltd.,1963

to get there, and that means two short bus rides—the Broadview bus and the Leaside bus.

To amuse myself while waiting for this second bus, which never seems to arrive, I stare at Don Mills United Church on that Pape and O'Connor corner. The sign, in particular, "Sunday services at 10 a.m." raises my Catholic hackles.

My mind is off on a scolding tangent at this church that is not Catholic, and according to Catholic teaching, anyone who goes here is a "bad non-Catholic." I say none of this out loud. What will Mom think? She is a good Catholic, but she limits her religious fervour to fish on Fridays, fasting in Lent, and getting me to Sunday Mass.

I look up the street, but the bus still isn't visible at the turn in the road. When it finally arrives, we climb on board and ride the rest of the short trip to one block north of the Danforth. There the bus loops into dead-ended Lipton Street with a high stonewall at the end.

"You need new shoes, Sharon," Mom says as we exit the bus and take brisk steps to the Danforth. A few blocks west we enter Pollock's Shoe Store. I remember its outside walls were a dingy yellow brick, but if they could have kept me outside and away from the monster inside, they could have been dull grey or even invisible. At that point, my only interest is getting my feet fitted into new shoes.

After Mom and I sit in a couple of chairs, this clerk, a young male, comes over. After a few words with Mom, he tells me to remove my shoes, then directs me to this weird-looking machine that stands almost as high as me. It is a monster. But Daddy isn't here to keep it away. Just Mommy, sitting in a nearby chair, and this clerk mumbling something about x-raying my feet, telling me to step up close and slide my feet inside. He must notice my hesitation because he says in a louder voice.

"It's okay. It's only an x-ray machine, and it will take pictures of your feet so we know what size shoe you need."

Gingerly, I do as he says. Once my feet are inside, I notice a flat glass cover on the top, level with my chest. So I look down through it.

And wish I hadn't.

My feet have turned into skeletons. Am I dead? Where is Daddy when I need him?

I notice my hands still look normal, when the clerk says, "Size two. Let's measure the width." He points to the chair, and I remove my feet from the machine. My feet appear normal; at least I can walk back to the chair. Once seated, the clerk hauls out a wooden contraption, horizontal like a ruler, but wider and shaped more like an elongated foot sole, with a board sliding across its top. He gently places my right foot on the contraption, glides this board down to the tips of my toes, and adjusts the sides to my foot.

"She'll need a C, a medium-width shoe." The clerk nods at Mom.

I'm still staring at my feet.

So, I get new dress shoes, in white. But we buy the running shoes at Kresge's.

Kresge's, Woolworth's, and Metropolitan (The Met)—almost the whole she-bang of dime stores—occupy their separate spots covering over four blocks on the Danforth. Mom treats them like royalty, and going into the dime stores and trying on Easter hats is the only light during the dark days of Lent. I'm not an adult, so I have to suffer through every Friday's fish or scrambled eggs with tinned spaghetti. Mom, however, fasts. One day a week, she lives on coffee until suppertime. I could never see the point in fasting. Your stomach growls; you feel faint and act so stupid you would kill for a piece of cake, never mind the bread. When it's not one of Mom's fasting days, we have lunch at the counter at Kresge's or The Met—hot dogs and hot chocolate, the perfect eat-out lunch for a kid. Today, Kresge's and The Met are no more. Replacements such as Dollarama and Giant Tiger provide the 21st century version of the previous dime stores. Inflation has raised the roof on price—"dollar plus" is the present classification, although dimes are still part of the currency—at this point. Woolworth's has rolled into the mega Wal-mart stores where you can eat lunch, often at an in-store McDonald's.

When we've finished lunch, Mom and I head out to buy real food.

Like today, the Danforth flourished with green grocers selling fresh vegetables and fruit and a butcher's shop, although unlike today, the owners of the former were Italian, not Asian. Mom often bought a basket of peaches, plums or strawberries from the green grocers.

The butcher's shop captures my curiosity. Mom opens the door to a clanging bell; we step in, and my feet feel as if they're traipsing through Grandpa Charlie's barn. I stare down at…

"Sawdust," Mom says. "That's so the butcher can sweep the floors easier."

I don't see any pieces of meat there. As Mom grabs a number and waits her turn, I look up at the shoulder-high counters. Behind glass barriers lie slabs of meat in various hues of red and pink. I recognize only bacon, as I've seen its striped pink and white fat curling in the fry pan for Sunday breakfasts at home. My nostrils flinch at an unfamiliar odour mixed in with the sawdust, but this is not like the smell of the chickens bawk-bawking around in Grandpa's chicken room. This smell is more animal, more immediate and ripe, and I don't like it.

"A pound of medium ground," Mom says.

The butcher, wearing a blood-stained apron that one day was probably white, picks up stringy medium-red worms. I want to gag.

"For hamburger," the butcher says, with a big grin. Gulp! I need to get out *now*.

Of course, I eat hamburgers, as a kid, as a teenager, as an adult, including at McDonald's. They always have to be cooked, almost burned. When I am 50, I give up eating red meat for five years because it bothers my digestive system. I never get over the squeamishness of handling raw meat.

In August we make our annual August trek to the Canadian National Exhibition on the waterfront near Sunnyside. Usually it is just Mom and I, travelling the King Street car from Broadview and Danforth, right into the CNE grounds, then lining up at the small tent-like wicket to pay the admission. Mom never goes on the rides. With no siblings, I usually ride solo. Except the rare occasion when Daddy tags along.

Which he does when I am four and a half-years-old and learning to sail without sails. Daddy and I are squished into one of the small two-seater boats in Lake Non-existent on the midway. He is trying to steer. He doesn't drive cars, but isn't a boat different? He is my Daddy; he won't let me fall down below. My eyes follow the pole attached in the middle of the boat to the rafters above. Maybe someone is up there, keeping the vessels safe. The front of our boat broadsides another. I clench the seat as if that will keep my bottom from bobbing up and out. Daddy jerks the wheel, and we careen sharply to my right. I look up to the rafters. No one is there.

"It's okay, Sharon," Daddy says., smiling.

And suddenly it is.

I relax my clench—a little. Still I am relieved when we are off the boat and on a safer beast—the merry-go-round. I'm riding a ceramic horse, not quite cowboy, more *cirus au ballet*, as the platform swirls around, almost to the beat of the nursery rhyme filling the circle. This time, Daddy clutches the horse's pole as he stands on the platform, moving along in tandem with the "galloping" horses.

One August, Linda and Margaret come down to Toronto from the farm with my godmother. Cousin Brenda from Detroit is here as well. We drive in and, as Mom and I usually do, pick Food Day, the first Wednesday of the CNE. You can get free samples in the Food Building—cheese, cookies—but we focus on lining up for the 99-cent hamburger. And eating it once we get to the grill up front. I don't know why all the fuss about this hamburger—it is a flat skinny beast, sandwiched in between a thin white bun. But the juice buds inside my mouth salivate while I stand waiting and inhaling the smoky aroma of burgers sizzling on the grill. My eyes nearly pop at the knife rat-a-tatting through big fat tomatoes. Then I savour the burger, tomato slice, lettuce slab and bun, chunk by chunk.

Our family gets separated. The Food Building is crowded, and the grownups want to go in different directions. Mom and I stick together but then we can't find my godmother, Linda, and Margaret. Cousin Brenda is with us. We try to move through the crowds, jerking our heads around for familiar faces. We reconnect. Afterwards, I think we should have tied us all together with mitten strings.

But when it's just Mom and me, we stay close and, when we *have* to go home, stand in the crowds on the wide sidewalk by the tracks waiting for the King streetcar. I hang onto Mom's hand and see the Bathurst streetcars roll in. The crowd pushes forwarded to get on, and Mom tries to steer me out of the way. Finally, we board a King streetcar. Mom manages to snag a seat, and we squeeze in. I stare at the people packing air space from the floor to what seems like the ceiling. At Mom's "we don't get off until the other end," I close my eyes and doze until we reach Broadview and Danforth.

I don't know what endears me to old streetcars. Maybe it's the clang-clang of the streetcar announcing it is starting to move out of stalled traffic, the grinding of its steel wheels on metal tracks, or the screech as it whirls around corners.

I think it has something to do with Mom taking me on so many streetcar rides. Often we skipped the subway up Yonge Street and took the Queen streetcar east to Broadview, then switched to the King streetcar up to the Danforth. Or sometimes we'd walk down Yonge Street from Queen to King and do that King Street run (this time with my eyes open wide and staring out the window as the streetcar squealed across the bridge joining King and Queen Streets). Mom shepherding me around Toronto by TTC instilled in me the necessity, and even the right, to available public transport.

What Mom's guidance didn't do was smooth over the stopover at one of our family destinations.

9: Destination—City Cousins

The most basic human desire is to feel like you belong. Fitting in is important
—**Simon Sinek,** English Author

It is my first time here. As soon as Mom, Daddy, and I set foot inside *their* doorway, I get an urgent need to fit in. Mom has elevated Daddy's younger sister and her family to snooty level. Perhaps her attitude creeps into my subconscious. All I know is, once we step off the Bloor streetcar at Bathurst and start walking the block to the side street, I crawl inside myself. When Mom or Daddy knock on the front door of the three-story row house, I nearly choke on my shyness. It is like visiting the Queen, King, and their princesses.

I *have* to fit in with my French-Canadian Grandma Lou, with her daughter, Marion, Marion's husband, Monty, and the couple's three daughters, Felicity, Sarah, and Nina. I *have* to fit in on the several Christmas Days we spend there, although I have no recollection of Christmas dinner. Instead, the big event visiting on my first Christmas Day is a tea party for us girls and our dolls.

Of course, I bring along Patsy, my oldest doll. She is my only doll then, a big doll with yellow curls, but to me she is a princess. Until we sit down at the card table with Felicity, Sarah, Nina, and their dolly brood. The tabletop is spread with tea things, all in silver-tin. I feel lost in this whirl of girls with soft almost lisping voices, so I remain in quiet mode.

I gaze around the living room beyond the corner where we are sitting. The grownups are involved in their grownup talk, but my aunt sees me staring at the Christmas tree in the opposite corner. Three presents, like lost parcels, lie underneath the tree.

"Those are for Felicity," my aunt says. "Her birthday is December 26, so she can't open her birthday presents until tomorrow."

I almost feel sorry for this oldest cousin born much closer to Christmas than me.

But it is Nina, six months my senior, whom I gravitate towards. We aren't good friends, but despite the formalities of the tea party, we seem to click.

A few years later, when Nina and I are eight or nine, Mom, Daddy and I are again visiting, but it is in the spring. We are all seated around my aunt's dining room table, finishing our meal. Nina and I excuse ourselves to make merry upstairs. We charge up the two stairways, bobbing our left hands along the top of the heavy black railings, and sneak into Grandma Lou's two-room attic bedroom and kitchen/sitting room at the top. We take a quick look at the sloping ceilings and the cans of food neatly piled on open kitchen shelves. I lean up against the small table and wonder what Grandma Lou can fit in her tiny fridge, and if she even cooks on her small stove.

"Come on, Sharon," Nina says. "Let's go."

Nina and I are in snoop mode. We're both reading Nancy Drew and think we are smarter than Miss Drew. We have to get the goods on the grownups and Nina's older sisters, so we are going to spy on them. Nina collects lined paper and pencils, and we creep down the two flights of stairs to the second and third steps from the bottom. We sink down, one behind the other, peer between the railings and observe our elders in action.

"Hah, hah." Aunt Marion shakes her head. "That's priceless." Her gravelly voice carries over to us. Nina and I start scribbling.

Aunt Marion is laughing. Julia is scratching her nose, I write. *She still has some food on her plate. Daddy is looking at his watch. Uncle Monty is looking over at the stairs.*

Nina and I duck lower.

"Where are Nina and Sharon?" Uncle Monty asks.

"Oh, Daddy, they're just upstairs playing," says Felicity.

"Hmrpmph," he says; then turns to Daddy. "Do you want more beer, Albert?"

He nods his head. Uncle Monty moves his chair back from the table and stands up. He is heavy and tall, like a giant. He stomps towards the kitchen.

The kitchen doorway is right in front of Nina and me, so we swivel around and half crawl, half walk up the stairs. We look back. Uncle Monty glances up at us. We look down, then up. He just shrugs his shoulders and enters the kitchen. Nina and I stare at each other and giggle.

We can't really nail our parents and her older sisters for anything beyond drinking beer (the adults), talking, and not finishing lunch, something Mom would never let me get away with.

One summer, Nina comes to spend a few days with me. Mom has bought foot-long hot dogs which waggle out a couple of inches at each end of the buns. She heats the wieners in boiling water in the top of the double-boiler pot, sticks them between the buns, and plasters on mustard, relish, and ketchup. Nina and I plunk them on plates and take them outside on the veranda. We're sitting in the Muskoka chairs, munching on the dogs when The Bully and her next-to-our-age sister, Shannon, stroll up the street and turn into our driveway. I start talking to The Bully like she is my best friend.

"How are you? This is my cousin, Nina. Nina's mother and your mother know each other from school or something."

"Hello, Nina," The Bully says.

Nina remains silent.

"Do you want to join us for hot dogs and then play with us?" I ask The Bully and her sister.

Nina bolts into the house. What's all this? She can't be shy. Shyness is my territory. I follow her into the house.

"Don't you want to play with my friends?" I ask her.

"No." She cowers on the chesterfield.

Nina is company, so I have to treat her that way. I go outside and make some excuse to The Bully. She and her sister leave. It never occurs to me that maybe Nina senses what I can't seem to grasp—The Bully is bad news;

she contaminates her surroundings, changing peacefulness into a war zone. Does Nina sense this? Is that why she wants to avoid her at all costs?

Part Three: The Hard Knocks Of Learning

Sharon Age 10 in Holy Cross School Uniform

A Sample of Sharon's Childhood Books

10: Mom's Eight Rules of Honesty

People who are brutally honest get more satisfaction out of the brutality than out of the honesty

—Richard J. Needham

"Eat your dessert or the police will come and get you," Mom says. She points to the front door and nods her head like I better do it or else the Black Maria will roll up the driveway and scoop me up into its dark interior.

I stare down at my bowl. Stewed huckleberries and apples. Black smashed berries and their dark juice seep through the apples. Yuck. Smothering the stew in vanilla ice cream can't hide the taste of huckleberries, a taste that sits in the middle between sweet and bitter. But Mom insists on growing these strange berries in her garden.

"Sharon, did you hear me?" Mom gets up from the kitchen table, scurries into the living room and stares out the front window. "Oh, I can see a police car coming up the street; it's turning into the driveway."

I start to shovel the mixture down my throat. Then I jump up and take my turn at the living room window. Down the street, Marie's father cuts his front lawn; Mrs. Armstead sits on her front veranda with her collie dog at her feet, and a couple of finned cars cruise up the road towards the dead-end street. Our driveway at 139 lolls in its usual empty state. When I finally get the nerve to look straight down at the veranda outside the window, all I see are the two green Muskoka chairs—empty.

Such was my mother's twist of the truth. My legacy is rich with the fallout from her Rules of Honesty. She had a skewed sense of right and wrong. According to Mom, *I* had to tell it all as it actually happened, but she could tailor *her* honesty according to what she thought suitable for little ears to hear or what she wanted little people to do. Or she could stretch the truth by throwing in a little imagination. I compare it to a ruler, each inch (or centimetre, depending on your generation) from one to eight being the equivalent of one of Mom's Rules of Honesty to live life. The higher the ruler number doesn't necessarily mean the more significant the rule. So, in no order of importance, here are Mom's Rules of Honesty. Rules I learned to live with.

Let's put down the police/dessert fiasco as Rule Number 1. When you want someone to do what you say, use a little imagination, and twist the truth. If you break the law, the police will arrest you, refusing to eat your unjust desserts is a crime.

Mom's Rule Number 2 and Rule Number 3 deal with The Bully. Excluding my forays into rulers and rocks, I usually suffer The Bully's torture in silence. That corners me into Mom's Second Rule of Honesty—rat on someone and you will be rewarded.

In Grade 3, The Bully sits right in front of me. When Mrs. Roberts isn't looking, The Bully swivels around and talks to me out of turn. However, her biggest sin is cheating with the numbers. When we complete an arithmetic exercise, Mrs. Roberts says "trade." The Bully crouches over my assignment, purses her lips, picks up her pencil and scribbles—x, x, x—beside my correct answers. Meantime, I, blessed with my mother's streak of honesty, also mark x, x, x, but alongside The Bully's incorrect answers. When we trade back, The Bully crouches even lower and turns the x's into $\sqrt{}$'s. At home, I whine to Mom.

"You have to tell the teacher when she cheats," Mom says. She's sitting in the chair under the living room window, and I'm standing in front of her as if I am the bad girl in school. "Next time, she cheats, tell the teacher. Then tell me, and I'll give you a quarter."

Money talks. The next time The Bully messes up the math marks I raise my hand and rat. When I return home, I tell tales out of school and claim my reward, not just 25 cents, but my admission to the honesty/money see-saw.

Once enveloped in her groove, Mom couldn't leave this Bully thing alone, but I did try to learn Rule No. 3—sometimes it is better to lie by omission than bare all. Often, it was difficult figuring out when to make this choice.

Take the business with the back lanes.

On the way to school, a laneway stretches for two blocks. The first block from the school runs behind bungalows, the second block behind the shops—the IGA Grocery Store, Hurst's Pharmacy, Donland's Movie Theatre, Donland's Restaurant, Chainway Dime Store, and various convenience stores, hair salons, and barber shops that make up the East York suburban shopping block in the 1950s and early 1960s.

"Don't take the laneway," Mom says. "There are tramps, bad men who want to hurt little girls there."

Of course, when The Bully cajoles me into walking through the laneway, I follow. Defying her fills me with more terror than what we might find in the laneway—perhaps bad men with horns leaping out of the alleyways between the rear of the stores. The most we see are a couple of men unloading a truckload of food behind the IGA. I make it home safely.

"Did you take the laneway?" Mom asks.

Swallowing saliva, I mumble a "no." The next walk through won't be just The Bully dragging me along behind the stores, but a big chunk of guilt.

Occasionally a smidgeon of family truth, the real truth, not the police story, surfaced.

Consider Mom's unacknowledged feud with Aunt Marion. Behind their backs, but in front of little ears, Mom called Marion and her family "snooty," but I think she felt a little unsure of herself. The plain farm girl who snagged Dapper Albert could never become buddy-buddy with his sleek younger sister. Then there was the funeral of an aunt by marriage on Daddy's side, which Marion "forgot" to tell my mother about—or so Mom let slip a few years later. At the time of the funeral, I remember that I overheard Mom yelling at Marion on the phone.

Based on the above, Rule Number 4 is thou shall not hide deaths in the family from the family. The truth will out in the obituary. The results are bad temper and bad feelings; neither makes good glue to hold together a family.

Rule Number 5 is showing your truth by your actions. Mom didn't usually demonstrate her affection for her family, except occasionally hugging me. Instead her actions showed the words she couldn't speak. Although not a trained nurse, she followed what the Catholic religion taught—"minister to the sick." When I suffered chest colds, she prepared a poultice to clear my chest. I don't recall my parents demonstrating affection for each other, but later when the evil within would attack Daddy, she would be the first at his side.

Hand-in-hand with showing your truth by your action is Rule Number 6—realize that everyone's truths don't necessarily jibe. That hard lesson will be my take-away when Daddy gets sick, a lesson that will howl at me repeatedly in years to come. But for my first 10 years, it will be kept at bay, despite all the forewarnings of family sickness and deaths. Not in our house—they just happened outside its walls.

Instead, we lived by the opposite—Mom's Rule Number 7—give honestly from the heart; do not have a hidden agenda.

After Uncle Stanley died, and my godmother was left with seven children to raise, someone else besides her nearby family and friends stepped up to help—my Mom. She couldn't be physically present 24/7—she had Daddy and me to look after in Toronto, plus the house and garden, and her sister lived miles away on the farm near Wingham, Ontario.

But we had Canada Post.

The sisters write back and forth a lot, and Mom sometimes shows me my godmother's letters, but not her replies. Instead she makes a big fuss out of playing Goodwill to help her younger sister.

When the snow piles up in Toronto and stacks up on the farm, boxes of hand-me-downs, mother's old clothes, my no-longer fitting clothes, and as suspected in hindsight, some store-bought ones, find their way from our house to theirs.

Rule Number 8 is telling the truth when you know it will get you into trouble because lying or staying silent just doesn't seem right. Long before the hippie movement promoted letting it all hang out, I practised this rule.

A few years before the Don Valley Parkway springs up, my new best friend, Barbara, her mother, and I go hiking in the Don Valley. Mom packs peanut butter sandwiches, an apple, and milk in a thermos and hands them to me with a warning.

"Don't go in the Don River."

I don't know why she is fixating on this. Mom came with me when I hiked before with the Brownies in the Don Valley. True, we didn't wade in the water, but we trekked through tall grass, deep woods, and, every time we saw a hole, I figured a snake was curled inside. So, why is Mom giving me this warning now? Is she listening to her eccentric sister, Gretchen, who harps on everything from fluoride water to Communism? Maybe Gretchen has moved into bad river water or maybe Mom remembers the muddy hue of the Don when we did the Brownie hike. Or maybe she is concerned because I never learned to swim.

So, when Barbara, her mom, and I go hiking in the Don Valley I am determined not to stick even toes in the Don River. The hike is an eye-opener, from learning to pee in the bush, to avoiding the Don River by crossing on tree trunks joining the land on either side of the Don.

"Come on, you just walk across it like this," Barbara says, as she hops on the dead trunk sprawled across the river and starts walking.

"I'll fall in," I say.

"Oh for heaven's sake," her mother says. "Just sit on it and move yourself along it." She demonstrates. "Well, come on." She turns around and looks at me, a slight woman, her lined face scrunched into a scowl and her short dark hair hidden under a safari hat.

The trunk feels softer than presumed, but it is dead, and I am afraid that it might crumble. Barbara has already reached the other side. Was that a smirk on her face? I slide my bum onto the log, but make sure my hands remain on it, too. The trunk stays put so I lean forward and gently bob my way forward. Barbara's mom does the same, and, despite the two of us bumming along simultaneously, I am amazed that the trunk doesn't budge. Still scared when we reach the other side, I sigh with relief. This scenario might explain why Barbara's mom insists we wade the next time we have to get to the other side. She and Barbara are already removing their shoes and socks, when I launch into my protest.

"I can't. My mother told me not to go in the Don River."

"Well, there's no log nearby, and that's the only way we're going to get across. Look it's not deep." Barbara's mother steps into the river, and it is up to her ankles. She turns around; she looks like a bird ready to pounce, so I sit on the river bank, remove shoes and socks, stuff the socks in the shoes, and, with one in each hand, step into the Don. I stand up to mid-calf. The water is warm, and I try not to look at the colour—a muddy brown green.

I arrive safely to the other side. We didn't bring towels, so we sit around and wait for our feet to dry before putting shoes and socks back on. Once shoed, we make our way out of the valley and exit onto Don Mills Road, just a few laps away from the stairs leading up to the dead-end street. Now I stand on familiar ground because this is something I have done without tattling to Mom. With my friends, I have climbed from the dead-end street onto busy Don Mills Road, darted across, and taken the back way into the park facing O'Connor Drive. Mom used to rant about staying off the stairs and Don Mills Road, but I ignored her warning and never told her.

Barbara and her mom walk me back home, and, after we say our goodbyes, I head inside.

"How was your hike?" Mom asks. "Did you go into the Don River?"

"Yes," and now I'm in for a lecture about the Don being unclean. I feel dirty. But I told the truth.

Mom also used to say she had no tact, Despite this and her eccentric take on honesty, she sowed the seeds of diplomacy and justice in me, two seeds that took a long time to germinate. For many years , when opening my mouth, I suffered from foot-in-mouth disease.

Mother's honesty didn't just encompass telling the truth; it covered people's basic integrity and how they dealt with the screw-ups, bad times, and bad luck that always pop up in life. The trick is to wind yourself through the days, months and years until you die—without falling into the muddy waters.

Maybe I should have learned to swim with the sharks, like The Bully.

11: Tales In and Out of Grade School

No one can look back on his school days and say with truth that they were altogether unhappy.

—**George Orwell**

We climb the back stairs, The Bully in front, with me behind. I am hoping we don't run into any of the teachers. *I forgot my speller* I will say if we meet anyone. We round the bend in the staircase and continue up. My little legs are beginning to tire. At the top of the stairs, The Bully moves towards the first classroom on the right. The door is open. She strides in, and I follow. This is not our classroom. She starts walking the perimeter, then the narrow aisles between the desks. Of course, I am right behind.

Then we hear it.

"I'll be right with you. I'm just going to pick up my books."

"Teacher," The Bully whispers as the click-click of heels moves towards the classroom doorway...

***

Classes have finished for the day, but the two of us are engaged in one of our snoop and hide tactics. For some reason we're hanging around the school. One of us has to go into the school for something, maybe to use the washroom. But once inside, The Bully decides we have to explore the coat closets for each classroom...

These closets are not identical. The four classrooms on the first floor share one large walk-in cloakroom, which by cloakroom standards is large—its length is the width of a classroom, but its narrowness is further compromised when cluttered with boots lying every which way on the floor, with coats, hats, jackets and leggings swelling out from the hooks or piled on the floor over the boots. The smell of damp rubber and hot radiator steam is enough to put your nose out of joint and either drive you crazy hunting through clothing paraphernalia for your mittens, or right out the door to breathe. That late afternoon, when The Bully opens the cloakroom door and we poke our heads in, it is empty except for a stray jacket, a pair of boots, one mitten, and the radiator discharging its fetid vapour.

However, when we explore inside a classroom on the next floor we run into teacher trouble…

…The Bully gallops towards the closet in the back. With its four doors it appears large for a classroom closet. When we close the doors from inside, we are standing in a dark and confined space. We dare not say anything. My heart thuds, and breathing is difficult. I am sure the teacher will discover us. From the other side of the closed doors, reverberate sounds of papers rustling, heels tapping, a door squeaking; then silence.

The Bully pushes the door open and charges out, followed by me, a little more discreetly. No one is in the hall. We leave, anyway. I suspect she was as scared as me. Perhaps for that moment in the closet, we were in sync, friends, not enemies.

A rare school moment…because usually when The Bully sticks her nose into my business, bad things happen and spiral into more bad things, sometimes dragging in other kids and teachers.

The chaos seems to start when The Bully and I move up to full days in Grade 1, after our mothers scrap the chaperon. Four times a day, including lunchtime, The Bully and I do the 15-minute jaunt to and from school, often accompanied by other classmates dawdling up Donlands. Some like Robbie, Gerry, and Linda turn west along O'Connor, but Tom, the strawberry thief, continues on with The Bully and me. The Bully teases me, and I'm too timid to tell her off. But Tom does.

"Leave her alone," he says.

That doesn't give him the green light to take strawberries from Mom's garden without her permission.

In class, he sits kitty-corner in front of me and listens as The Bully taunts me. I blink to try to keep the tears inside. Tom swings around and stares mournfully at me with his baby blue eyes.

"Don't cry," he says.

But plenty makes me cry.

The grade school classrooms were breeding grounds for the mores of the 1950s. These standards permeated my mind and not only affected me then, but remained pending, ready for later retrieval when I least expected it.

At the core stood our Catholic religion. Its ensnaring tools were the Baltimore Catechism, which had been around since 1884 when the Catholic plenary council in Baltimore, Maryland baptized it into existence. The words soon spread into Canada and other countries and didn't ease off until the mid-1960s,[14] long after my young vulnerable mind had swallowed its plateful of questions and answers. All by rote.

Catholicism's top enforcer in my world is Father M., pastor at Holy Cross.

He plods into our classroom up to the front. He is old, white-haired, and he glares at us as if we are Lucifer's darlings. Then he opens his mouth

"You are all big fat zeroes," he says.

Silence.

He repeats this with each visit. At Sunday Mass, he mounts the pulpit, glares down at us, and begins his sermon the same way.

It has a profound effect on a shy only child. I begin to feel as if my ideas are worthless, unless I get confirmation and approval from "authorities" such as my parents, teachers, or the priests. Confessions, for me, often include "Is it a sin if you...?"

Confessions become a monthly way of life for us at Holy Cross after our First Communion in Grade 1. For that Communion Day, I stride up

---

[14] Palmo, Rocco. *Whispers in the Loggia*. "Why Did God Make You?" [Accessed August 19, 2020]. http://whispersintheloggia.blogspot.com/2007/04/why-did-god-make-you.html

the church aisle in my child-bride white dress with veil trailing; outfit, courtesy of Mom's sewing skills, ceremony, orchestrated by the Catholic Church and its teaching cohorts. Following the Communion breakfast (bacon, eggs, and toast) in the church basement, Mom snaps photos of The Bully and me outside the front of 139.

After that, the day before the first Friday of the month, our current teacher marches us over to the church to tell all behind closed curtains. We are sinners, and we need our sins erased so we can go to Holy Communion with a clear conscience the next day. Sins are divided into mortal (very bad, like murdering your brother), or venial (smaller sins, like telling white lies about your brother). Two priests await us, one in each of the two confessionals. If we're lucky, we line up in the larger group outside the assistant priest's confessional. If not, we shake and battle butterflies in our stomachs while waiting our turn to confess all to the pastor. The sojourn seems to stretch for hours, as each victim-to-be contemplates the ordeal ahead.

I stumble into the pastor's confessional. My heart is galloping and my mind cannot get past the inevitable stern lecture.

"Bless me, Father, for I have sinned," I say. "It has been two weeks since my last confession. I…I…er, I disobeyed my mother. I told two lies…" My litany continues.

Then I'm in for it. Father M. lectures me on why I should be truthful and obey my parents. Father M.'s words sink into my mind, my heart, and my soul. His voice is a loud whisper, and I just know everyone outside will hear and find out my secret—I am the biggest, the fattest zero in Holy Cross parish. If Father M. doesn't absolve my sins, I will go to hell in something faster than a hand basket.

"I absolve you of your sins," Father M. says. "For your penance, say 10 Our Fathers and 10 Hail Marys." He makes the cross sign. "Go in peace and sin no more." He slides the window partition shut.

I grab the small ledge, peel my knees from the wooden kneeler, and wobble up. When pushing open the curtain, I feel relief. Saying my penance will keep me safe and clean...until the next time. Fingering the rosary in my hands as if it is a talisman, I hurry to the sanctuary railing. I take my time with the Our Fathers and the Hail Marys. When finished praying, the shaking has disappeared, replaced by a rumbling stomach. I walk purposely down the front aisle to the back of the church, out the door, and continue on home for lunch, alone for a change.

Friday morning, I wake up earlier than usual for school, because first I'm headed for the 8 a.m. Mass. I can't eat before Holy Communion, so Mom fortifies me with a packed breakfast—cold scrambled egg sandwiches, an apple, and hot chocolate in a thermos. I can never get the thermos open, so in class where we all sit after church to eat breakfast,—I swallow my embarrassment and walk to the front.

"I can't get it open," I say to the teacher. He or she always can.

When the teacher was Mother St. Helen, (nuns were called "Mother," not "Sister") my anxiety vaulted to near Father M. level. Mother St. Helen was a young nun with a small pointed nose and red hair poking out the top of her veil. She had the temper and severe look to match, and I wonder if she took stern lessons from Father M. I had her for Grades 2 and 8.

In Grade 2 we applied our Grade 1 reading skills in exercises.

"Turn to page 12, exercise A." Mother St. Helen stands behind her desk. She holds the exercise book, alternating between glancing down at it and over at us. "When you are finished it and exercise B, quietly bring them up for me to look at." She sits down.

For the next 15 to 20 minutes the only sounds are the flipping of pages and the scratching of pencils. I read through each question and write down my answer, or draw the picture required. Some of the students finish quickly and line up at Mother's desk, so now I hear her occasional, "That's wrong. How do you expect to pass Grade 2?" and "Good."

I have now completed the work, so I pick up the exercise book, which is the size of a thick colouring book, walk to the front and line up. Nora and Mickey stand in front of me. Mother looks at Nora's work and says, "Good."

I think I also have done all right.

"How do you expect to pass Grade 2?" Mother asks Mickey.

I hope I have done all right.

It is now my turn. I say nothing while placing the open exercise book before Mother. She presses her lips together as she follows along on the page with her pencil. When she reaches the bottom, she jerks the book at me.

"What's this?" she asks.

I look down and read out loud. "Draw an X."

"The word isn't 'X.' It's an 'axe.'"

I have drawn an "X."

"Stupid," she says. "You should know better than that." She whacks the pencil against my nose.

Tears well up in my eyes. My face must be turning red because Mother looks strangely at me.

"I'm sorry. Did I hurt you? Come down to the lunchroom after school, and I'll make it up to you."

I can't speak because I am too busy pretending tears are not sliding down my face.

Later, taking slow exaggerated footsteps down to the basement, I have no idea what to expect. Before today, I steered clear of the nuns' lunchroom, rushing by it when heading for the girls' washroom in the same alcove. Today, I make a pit stop there, tip-toe over to the lunchroom, and stare at the dark brown door, expecting Mother St. Helen's face to appear in the small curtained window near the top. I shuffle to the door.

Did the curtain just move? Swallowing saliva, I raise my right hand and knock lightly.

The door slides open.

Mother St. Helen wears a navy blue-and-white striped bib apron over her habit. She isn't smiling but the stern look has disappeared.

"Come in," she says.

Swallowing again, I enter behind her.

I don't remember what else she says, just a long speech of apology. Instead, I am fascinated by the layout of the room –small square table in the middle, tiny fridge, four-burner gas stove of the 24-inch variety, two stainless steel sinks, joined. At home, our sink has two separate taps but only one white porcelain basin. Above the sink is the only window, adorned with dark brown and green curtains in a flowered pattern.

Mother opens one of the chocolate brown cupboard doors over the counter. What now? She hauls out a tin. Cookies? She opens it and hands me a few pieces of wrapped candy.

She leaves the school after Christmas. Word has it she is sick. Years later I figure she had a nervous breakdown. But in that Grade 2 class it feels as if someone has removed a life sentence. In Mother's place arrives a sweet old lady, Mrs. Shorn. She is no-nonsense, but kind.

Mother St. Helen and I were not done yet. However, before our return match I would learn to play baseball, win at spelling bees, and tutor another student in Arithmetic.

In Grade 3, we girls discovered baseball—not the New York Yankees, but the unnamed Holy Cross Girls recess-and-after-school teams. By then the school had grown too small for the ever-expanding offspring of the baby boom, so the school board brought in three portables and dumped them in a corner of the girls' yard. You could find a brother or sister of most of my classmates in a portable or in the main building. As an only child, I was in the minority. That may explain why I adopted baseball almost like an obsession. Baseball was a way to belong.

The girls play in the schoolyard on one side of the school and the boys on the other. The twain never meet officially until Grade 8 when Mother St. Therese decides we should have a joint baseball match in the boys' yard. I stand, bat in hand, with my back to the school wall and wait for Jim to throw the ball. He does a Mickey Mantle wind-up, and sends the ball flying towards me. I swing at air. Where did the ball go? My head spins and the rest of me is rooted to the ground. I want to go back to playing with girls only on the other side of the school. At least then I can use my baseball quirks to make my way around the field.

Our girls' baseball diamond, a mixture of sporadic sand pits and weed patches, stands over by the three portables, so we have to be careful we don't throw or hit the ball through a window. That never happens, although some of those foul balls land between the portables or on one of their verandas. Not any I ever throw do. I play third base, over by the last portable near the linked fence corner. Whenever someone hits a ball my way, I catch it. This feat makes up for my lousy pitches. I can't strike anyone out even with my eyes open.

But I can hit—not far—just enough to run to first base. I am right-handed in everything else, but my technique is to hold the bat over my left shoulder and when I see the ball coming, swing the bat around and whack—when I don't miss.

After the girls and boys have that supervised baseball match, some of the guys take it to after school—in the girls' yard. We play workup baseball. Red is up to bat, and I stand on first base, not third. I watch Red swing the ball, watch it zoom, and plunk into my left cheek.

It hurts. I remember Mom's Rule Number 2 of Honesty—rat—because I charge into the principal's office and complain bloody murder; at least it must sound like I think Red is trying to kill me. Of course, it is an accident, but the boys really aren't supposed to play in the girls' playground. I go home, but guess Red gets into trouble. The hit doesn't stop me from playing baseball, though.

In winter, when snow, slush, and ice makes chasing after balls somewhat dangerous, we sometimes spend recess sliding down the small hill at the front end of the girls' yard, at the fence over by the church yard. When we are a few years older we will stand around in a huddle and talk.

In grade school I also develop my passion for reading. I progress from learning to read phonetically in grade 1, to reading those *See Jane Run* books, to the Bobbsey Twins, Hardy Boys, Nancy Drew, Trixie Belden, and to classics like *Black Beauty*, *Uncle Tom's Cabin*, and the *Little Women* books. Mom buys me all these latter ones, although we don't own many books.

Around the same time, reading leads me into something more. I enter the ranks of school browner and become the class Spelling Bee Queen. In those days we don't venture onto nation-wide TV spelling bees—we don't venture outside the class to spell. But 99 per cent of the time I win the bees. I have my way, without cheating (or killing my opponents), of getting around difficulties to do so.

Unlike the national spelling bees today, where the speller has to repeat the word to make sure he or she has the correct one, we just spell it out.

"Deceived," Mrs. Roberts calls out.

"D—e—c—e—i—v—e." I pause and stare at Mrs. Roberts. As she opens her mouth to disqualify me, I add, "d."

I am still in and remain to win at the end.

Unfortunately, my winning streak does not carry into the summer. When I am eight and a half, Mom decides to sign me up for swimming classes at one of our area high schools. She is so insistent, she walks with me to and from the classes for girls. But the girls are teens and much farther along in swimming lessons than me. Despite wearing ugly bathing caps that make my face resemble a moon, the water still manages to sting my ears. Later I will learn the culprit was the chlorine in the water. Maybe Aunt Gretchen's damnation of treated water had a point.

The next summer, after Grade 4, Mom decides to switch high schools for swimming classes and arranges with Marie's and Susie's mothers for the three of us to go together. Each weekday morning, Marie and Susie knock on my door, and we walk just over a mile from 139 to Danforth and Greenwood. This is the era when Volkswagens—the little yellow and green Beetles and vans begin monopolizing Toronto's streets. To amuse ourselves, the three of us call out "Volkswagen" whenever a Beetle or a van whizzes by. We give points for who sees the most; vans are worth more points.

We wear our bathing suits under our shorts and t-shirts, so when we arrive, we drop the last two items, our towels and underwear, into the changing room and head for the pool.

The pool scares me—it is big, deep, and every time I stand at the shallow end, I'm bobbing around and expect to lose my balance, slide underwater, and drown. I hate putting my face under the water and holding my breath. When the instructor decides we are going to learn to float, I want to disappear—anywhere but underwater.

We begin by hanging onto the side of the pool, lifting our legs up behind us until we are flat out, and letting our bodies coast. The instructor escalates the criteria. We duet, taking turns hanging onto our partner and stretching out. We kick; next float, first hanging onto our partner, then trying it on our own.

On the way home, Susie and Marie are all over me.

"Sharon is a scaredy-cat. Won't even let go to float."

I am hurt, feel stupid and inferior, and want to quit the lessons.

"No, you can do it," Mom says as she gives me a hug. Her big arms encircling me give me momentary comfort, so I decide to continue with the swimming classes.

Not for long. Indirectly, Mom is the cause of my quitting.

At the high school, Marie, Susie, and I share a change room, a small dark cubicle with a grey wooden bench at the back, grey walls toilet-stall height, and a door with a hook to lock it. On this particular Monday morning, the class is especially humiliating. I just *know* all eyes are on stupid little me as I gingerly try to float on my stomach while hanging onto the instructor. Everyone else has progressed to their backs. Afterwards, I try to hide in the cubicle. I want out, the faster, the better, so I yank all my clothes from the shopping bag, and what's this?

The underpants don't look like mine. Where did these come from? Did I pick them up from somewhere without realizing it? They look too big and are pressed. In my anxious state I forget that Mom irons everything, so I believe the pants belong to someone else.

"Whose are these? Are they yours?" I ask Marie and Susie.

"No," they both reply.

I'm holding onto them and staring at them. I can't wear someone else's pants, so I leave them behind and dress in my shorts, undershirt, and t-shirt. Now I stand at 100 per cent on the humiliation scale, especially as Marie and Susie seem to be getting close. They chatter to each other, leaving me out and walking home behind them.

"I'm not going back," I tell Mom when walking in the door, but don't tell her about the underpants. I now realize they are mine. "Marie and Susie pick on me because I'm stupid and too slow."

My feelings finally sink in with Mom. The next swimming day, when Marie and Susie knock on the door, Mom applies her Rule No. 1 in honesty.

"Sharon is sick and she won't be going swimming anymore," I hear her say from my bed.

I am not sick, just hiding. But swimming won't be the only hidden element during this summer of 1958. The other one is bigger, more far reaching.

12: The Enemy Within Starts Surfacing

Surely the best way to meet the enemy is head on in the field and not wait till they plunder our very homes.

—Oliver Goldsmith

On a cold day in late November 1958, Daddy packs his bag and takes public transit to Toronto Western Hospital, on Bathurst Street, a few blocks south of his "Dapper Albert" days. It is five months after his 59th birthday and three months since August when he had his annual chest x-ray.

I remember hearing my parents whispering in the hallway outside my bedroom several times as summer turns into fall. Somewhere in between x-ray and hospital, Mommy finally speaks up.

"Your Daddy has tuberculosis," she says, stopping me in the kitchen. "He has to go into the hospital, probably for an operation. But he'll be fine. TB is curable."

She is my mother, so I believe her.

Daddy stays in a ward. The room feels hot and putrid from the radiators belching out steam. But there is no real warmth, only frightened men, up to 80 years of age, their beds lined up college-dorm-style, 15 on each side with white curtains in between, serving as doors and walls to privacy. The real walls wear old green paint and the wood in the floors is dark oak; I suppose today we would consider the wood as classic. The ward gives the impression of being sparse and drab.

These men have various diseases and move and cough with varying intensity, or they huddle in their beds like statues lying on slabs, waiting to be propped up as tombstones. The man in the bed next to Daddy is an anomaly, 20, French Canadian, dark-haired, handsome, the first man I have a crush on. I am now nearly 10 going on 16. His right hand is consumed with gangrene and he will lose the whole hand if it doesn't get better, he tells us in halting English. I smile, blush, and keep my mouth shut. Maybe I'm visiting Daddy to see the French fellow, or am I really sitting in a chair between the two, with my eyes cast down, just to see Daddy? Certainly, Mom and I feel a whoosh of relief when we leave the hospital early the morning after Daddy's operation.

"He'll be okay," Mom says. "They removed half a lung."

The early morning air seems to feel so fresh, so new, as we walk from the hospital to the streetcar stop to go home.

"The good news," Daddy later says as he recuperates in the hospital, "is I can still drink. The bad news is I can't smoke anymore."

The good news continues. Daddy returns home and a few weeks later goes back to work, so I am lulled into complacence. He is still the king looking out for his little princess. That now includes making sure I get all my daily reading material.

I turn 10 December 1. With beginning the double-digit ages, my reading interests have expanded to the news in the city newspapers. .When Daddy arrives home from work, he brings the later edition of the *Toronto Daily Star* into the house and adds it to the pile in the kitchen. I think he is doing it just for me. Like a gambler drawn to a poker game, I am hot on Daddy's heels, reading the front page.

The front page of this *Toronto Daily Star* for March 10, 1959 headlines a story I probably should never have read. Twelve-year-old Patricia Lupton, supposedly en route to a babysitting job never came home.

Patricia Lupton was a 12-year-old girl living in Scarborough who along with three friends answered a blatant ad on the bulletin board at their local A&P Supermarket. The ad asked for babysitters to apply. All four girls had babysitting experience in their neighbourhood. So they did something you should never do—filled out all their contact information on the posted form. A few weeks later, Patricia received a phone call from a man calling himself "Mr. Johnston." He said he and his wife needed a babysitter that evening for their older son while they visited their younger offspring in the hospital. Patricia had a reputation as a reliable babysitter and was well-liked by the children she babysat and their parents. So, with her parents approval, and the promise to call them at 7 p.m., Patricia left for this babysitting job.

Patricia never called her parents. Patricia never came home. Four hours later her parents found out on what happened—from the news on CBC-TV. One hour after Patricia was supposed to meet "Mrs. Johnston" her body was found in a snowbank less than two miles from where she lived. She had been strangled with her own scarf.[15]

The story affects me so deeply that I seem to slide inside it, feeling an affinity with Patricia Lupton, but also feeling scared and shocked at a murder that happened in Toronto not too far from where I live. She is only two years older than I am. I don't mention the story and its affect to Mommy or Daddy.

The next day at school, Patricia's murder is the talk of the schoolyard at recess. Despite now being big girls in Grade 5, The Bully and I are scared. We notice police constables investigating something on the streets.

"They are looking for Patricia Lupton's murderer," The Bully says as she charges out of the schoolyard and onto the sidewalk. "What if the murderer is here?"

Cold fear shoots through me as I run after her.

"Are you looking for the murderer of Patricia Lupton?" she asks the officer walking towards us.

Fortunately, he does not tell us to mind our own business. Instead, he seems to notice our heightened state of fright. He explains that they are not here because of Patricia's murder, but something else. He also assures us

---

[15] Patricia Lupton Memorial, from *Find a Grave*, Online, [accessed July 9, 2020]
https://www.findagrave.com/memorial/9197068/patricia-lupton

that police are busy looking for her killer, but the killer is not in this area; he is not near our school, and we are safe to go back into our schoolyard.

It gives me a feeling of relief. Authority has spoken and quietened me. The Bully is also silent, for a change.

However, the murderer of Patricia Lupton would never be found, despite a cold case investigation by police years later. But it may have helped inspire me to read murder mysteries where the murderer always got his or her just desserts. And later, to write mysteries.

What I don't realize then is that The Bully and I have found some harmony once again, joining together in fear. Of course, this closeness is short-lived.

Soon after the Patricia Lupton scare, The Bully is back to her usual behaviour towards me. One cold day she chases me out of the schoolyard after school.

"Your Daddy has cancer." She taunts me between huffs and puffs. She waddles onto the sidewalk and tries to catch up to me.

"No, it was TB. You're lying." I glance at her over my shoulder, then my feet pick up the pace.

"Nah, your parents lied. My Mom said your Daddy has cancer."

She's lying. She's got to be lying. She seems closer to my back, so I detour into Holy Cross Church for solace.

"My mother said it was TB. My mother doesn't lie. Please God." I kneel on the wood-hard kneelers and hang onto the pew in front of me. "Please God. He had TB. My mother said so."

My pleading does not carve consolation into my heart. Instead, betrayal is born, and it grows as offshoots that make no sense at the time.

In those days, cancer wasn't so widespread, and like a dirty family secret, the adults kept it quiet from the children. Obviously, some of the neighbourhood kids knew. Like The Bully. Like Gregory, a friend from down the street. If I knew then what Gregory told me years later, would that have changed things? Would I have felt differently?

"Everyone on the street was upset that your father had cancer," Gregory said when we reconnected in 2012.

So everyone did know.

Except me.

Until a few months following Daddy's operation.

Part Four: Living With Devastation

Pink Piano and First Piano Book

Daddy's Last Photo 1965 Riverdale Hospital

13: Life Goes On?

Life is ten percent what happens to you and ninety percent how you respond to it.
— **Lou Holtz**, American Coach

Much later on I will realize that now I am coasting. Change can be ugly, and it is much safer to stay locked up inside my pea shell. Sure, Mom has to fess up—her lie goes way beyond the boundaries of her Rules of Honesty. As for Daddy, I don't think I consciously realize then how his cancer would affect our relationship. After all, he has returned to work, and I continue in school. He still brings in the daily newspapers and plunks them on the newspaper pile in the kitchen. However, there is no close bonding like before. There are no learning experiences from father to daughter, no big bicycles to learn to ride. A few opportunities slide in, but only one touches us on similar wavelengths. Strangely, Mom and I remain somewhat close.

School, however, continues to draw me in. The year of Daddy's lung cancer operation, the year I am in Grade 5, is the year where my teacher is my first male teacher.

But he isn't a father substitute. At 25, he is way too young for that. Despite his age, he seems to have the knack to figure out us 10-year-old kids. And we give him plenty to deal with: from Donald, hobbling in on crutches with two broken legs from falling off his bicycle near Tom's place, to David, sitting behind me, twirling my longish hair, and almost sticking it in the inkwell.

Mr. Bolt's class also introduces me to racial discrimination.

That year, a new student, Guenther, sits across from me in class. He is of German descent. Sitting behind him is Bernice, blond, white, of Scandinavian descent. On this particular day, she insults Guenther.

"Nazi," she calls him.

Mr. Bolt hears it. He stands up from his desk.

"What did you say?" he asks.

Bernice repeats it. Her voice is unsteady.

"The two of you, come up here," Mr. Bolt says to Guenther and Bernice.

They get up from their seats and walk to the front of the class. We all have necks and heads strained forward, and eyes and ears wide open.

"Now, face each other," he says.

The two comply.

"Now, Bernice, I want you to look at Guenther and apologize."

Bernice, close to tears and with head down, mumbles.

"Look at Guenther," Mr. Bolt says.

Bernice gives Guenther a tentative look.

"I'm sorry," she says.

The whole scenario affects me deeply. I am of German descent, too, but secretly have a crush on Guenther. Mr. Bolt's solution is much more humane, reasonable, and fairer than what I have read in *Uncle Tom's Cabin*.

Reading, however, does help me understand what occurs in math problems. It also helps if you know how to do addition, subtraction, multiplication, division, and fractions, which I learned in Grades 3 and 4. We had the multiplication tables drilled into us—orally, by rote. I was also good at written math, but as soon as it had to be done silently in my head, I became lost. It was like grabbing at air instead of numbers. They had to be seen to be calculated.

Mr. Bolt decides I can help some of the other students with their math. He pairs me with Concetta, one of the many recent Italian immigrants to Toronto. Concetta is age 13 to my 10. In the cold snowy winter, she stands on the sidewalk near the rest of us at recess. Dressed in a light coat, scarf, and slip-on shoes, her face wears a red bewildered look, frozen until she manages to open her mouth. The words jolt out like random sounds. I feel sorry for her. So, I welcome the chance to help her with her arithmetic.

Concetta and I tackle our addition, subtraction, and multiplication exercises on the blackboard at the front of the class while everyone else works at their desk. When I tutor Concetta, I lose any feelings of inadequacies; the only zeroes are the ones we write on the blackboard.

***

Back at home, changes are afoot. Daddy may have been well and working again, but something is off with Grandpa Charlie. That becomes obvious when he arrives for an extended visit to 139.

"Your Grandpa's having an operation at the hospital and he has to stay here awhile afterwards to get better," Mom says.

Mom reorganizes the layout of the land. Grandpa sleeps in the bigger bedroom; Mom bunks with me, and Daddy gets shuffled off to the new basement rec room where he sleeps on the roll-out cot. Nowadays, the company, not the married couple or even the kids, would get the shuffling.

Mom spends some time with Grandpa in the master bedroom.

"I have to help him change his dressing," she says.

Timidity doesn't halt my curiosity, so when Mom carries a basin of water, a washcloth and towel into the master bedroom, I enter my room, shut the door and squeeze up to the wall dividing the rooms. With my ear up close, I try to figure out just what is going on. Sounds like bandages tearing, water swishing, low voices talking, and then a loud, "Ouch," from Grandpa filter through the wall. This is serious business—Grandpa did have an operation. For some reason, I think it is his bladder.

Grandpa shuffles his feet in slippers through the house. Gone are the black boots, but the black trousers held up with suspenders and the white short-sleeved undershirt remain a part of his garb. However, something has changed. He is no longer in the wide-open spaces of the farm, and he needs to occupy himself. He sits in the living-room chair by the window and watches for me to come home from school. His eyes follow me as I walk up the driveway and climb the steps.

Mom moves the card table and a couple of chairs under the living room windows, and on warm sunny days, onto the front veranda.

Grandpa shuffles a pack of cards.

"Sharon, do you want to play 'Chase the Person Out of the Country?'" he asks.

"What's that?"

"Something like Fish and Hearts."

"Okay."

He deals—nine cards each.

"You have to collect all the other person's cards and chase them out of the country."

We go at it. Sometimes he wins; sometimes I win; but the game is not the purpose.

Although I look forward to these intervals spent with Grandpa, I won't realize until years later that his illness brought us closer in the little time he had left. Why can't a kid live an experience and just *know* in that moment how precious it is? However, Grandpa does return to the farm, now being run by Uncle Theodore, aided and abetted by Aunt Gretchen.

But in the chill of winter, on January 11, 1960, Grandpa dies. Mom won't let me go to the funeral because she is afraid I will get another earache, as happened when attending Grandma's funeral. Of course, Daddy has to stay home to look after me. This isn't the first family funeral in winter where Mom lays down her law, so you would think that Daddy and I would be used to it. An invisible aura of disappointment seems to emanate from him as he prepares our breakfast—frying eggs in a pan on the stove in the corner and popping bread into the toaster on the kitchen table. We don't say much, but seem to silently share our disappointment at not being able to go to Grandpa's funeral. I don't think it has quite sunk in that I will no longer see my Grandpa Charlie. I will no longer play Crokinole with him. We will also be visiting one less farm in the upcoming summer holidays. What doesn't sink into my pea shell, is the importance of Daddy and I silently in sync about not going to Grandpa's funeral. Grandpa is gone, but Daddy is still here…for the time being.

Meantime, I am now in Grade 6.

If I think Grade 2 with the crazy nun was peculiar, my Grade 6 teacher could give her competition in that department. Mrs. Keystone, near retirement age, reminds me of a clown when I look at her. Heavy face powder and eyebrow paint cannot hide her wrinkled face. But it is her eyes that command attention, at least to my newest friend, Leslie. She can't stop staring at Mrs. Keystone as the latter blinks her eyes a million times a minute. Leslie picks up her habit, which she doesn't realize until her mother points it out to her at home.

Mrs. Keystone's blinking eyes neither bother nor influence me, but something else about her does. She stands up to her short stature in front of the class, opens her red painted lips, and tells us many times.

"I will give credit where credit is due."

Those words, with my addition of "…and discredit where discredit is due" will become part of my credo for living as an adult.

For now, I focus on the mundane at school and at home. Daddy and I continue living in middle ground—neither close nor distant.

"Your friend from around the corner is moving," Mom says. She means The Bully, but I never call her that to Mom's face. They need a bigger house, Mom tells me, because a fourth child, another girl, has just been born.

I am surprised and not sure how to act. The Bully will be out of my life. Maybe Mrs. Keystone's axiom is working in my subconscious because I decide to say something to The Bully. One day she and I have another verbal run-in—what about, I can't remember. However, it sends her scurrying up one side of my street and me up the other side. I look across at her and in my loudest voice, yell:

"I'm glad you are moving away."

She turns, gives me a quick dirty look, then keeps on running—away from the street she lives on.

When September rolls around and we go back to school. *I won't have The Bully on my back. I will be free.*

But life has a way of throwing new situations at you and dragging out the unresolved. Often they don't mix. But what do I know?

Mommy and Daddy have come up with our dream summer vacation. We are headed for New York City. At 11 ½ I'm going to see the lights on Broadway.

The trip is filled with the highs of travelling the overnight train on a "foreign" railway and the scent and excitement of exploring a new world. But it is also a holiday supposedly taken within the confines of my parents' budget restraints and my barriers of timidity.

However, the day before we leave I get my first period.

"We can wait a few days or so to go," Mom says.

"No," I reply.

So, right on schedule, we climb aboard the CPR night train to New York City. We sit up the whole night, pillows propped behind our heads. Mom snores beside me and Daddy paces up and down the aisles and the corridors. I fall asleep, rocking to the rhythm of the train rolling along the rails until the movement jolts me awake to the eeriness of dimmed lights and still bodies. Then my eyelids slide shut and I am back coasting on this rollicking ride...

...Until morning when we take a taxi from Grand Central Station to our hotel. Mom and Daddy picked this hotel, the Waldorf Astoria, from an ad in the *Toronto Daily Star* and booked us there, sight unseen, for eight days.

The hotel is grand, gracious and gigantic— a true gem. Our large room has a double bed for Mom and Daddy and a single bed for me, as well as a big private bath. We have plenty of manoeuvring room and I don't feel strange sharing a room with Daddy.

During the late evening, I lie in bed, drifting in and out of sleep. Mom and Daddy are still up and I can hear their whispers.

"Too expensive for seven nights, Albert," Mom is saying.

"But, it's a nice hotel," Daddy replies.

I hear paper rustling and open my eyes. Mom and Daddy huddle over by the desk. Mom's hands are under the light from the lamp. She is thumbing through American greenbacks, every other second lifting her thumb to her mouth to wet it. Her mouth is moving and I realize she is counting. It is a quick count.

"We might be able to manage three nights here," she says, turning to Daddy. "But that's it. We have to check out and stay somewhere cheaper."

Daddy hauls out the phone book and they both seem to be studying some of its pages. I close my eyes and that is it for me until morning light.

The next morning we pack our bags and head downstairs. As Mom and Daddy do the checkout routine, I look around at the sparkling chandeliers overhead, the hushed carpets and the expensively-dressed hotel patrons. Although absorbing some of my parents' feelings of poor country mice, I could get comfortable here.

A taxi takes us to a second rate hotel, The Holland, at 351 West 42nd Street. Originally built in 1918 as a luxury women's residence, when my parents and I checked in, it hadn't yet deteriorated to its status as Manhattan's worst welfare hotel. That didn't occur until later in the 1970s and 1980s, when homeless people were housed in several older past-their-prime Manhattan hotels. The Holland acquired its reputation as worse than hell because it became a refuge for crack dealers, prostitution, vermin, unsanitary conditions, and an uncaring slum landlord. The landlord went bankrupt in 1985. After the formation of a tenant's association led by Thomas Reuter in 1987, plus the interest of Mayor Ed Koch's office and the Citizens Committee, the City bought the hotel and shut it down in 1988. The intention was to rebuild it as a state-of-the art residence for elderly welfare recipients and those with mental conditions. That happened in 1995 and it was renamed Holland House and divided into 40 apartments for the mentally ill, 40 for those with HIV/AIDS, and the rest for the homeless. At first Holland House changed the neighbourhood community and its property values[16] but by 2011 it had deteriorated into what a *New York Post*

---

[16] From *New York Times* archives and Project Renewal. Online. [accessed August 19, 2020],

story called a "flophouse."[17] On its 100th anniversary in March 2018 it received a boost—a 15 million dollar project renovation funded by the New York City Department of Housing Preservation and Development and was renamed Geffner House, after Ed Geffner, the former Project Renewal CEO[18]

Back in 1960, when my parents and I step into our room, the hotel can best be described as modest with no frills except the swimming pool in the basement. I don't swim, so we ignore it. Our room is tiny and my bed lives in the wall. Each night my parents press a button, and the bed springs out; it seems to fill the room. It is called a Murphy bed and if it is in any way related to Mr. Murphy of Murphy's Law, that fits our situation. The three of us almost trip over each other and the beds to move around. The bathroom is tiny and provides my only privacy from Daddy. I begin to resent him being there when I have to cope with my period. Every time I enter the bathroom, embarrassment rushes through me. I will have this nonsense for decades. I hate growing up.

I wish I were grown up every time I hear Roy Orbison sing "Only the Lonely," on the radio. I think of my latest movie-star crush, the Irish actor,

---

Freedman, Samuel G., "At Welfare Hotel, Tenants Group Gives Fragile Hope ," July 15, 1987
http://www.nytimes.com/1987/07/15/nyregion/at-welfare-hotel-tenants-group-gives-fragile-hope.html

Project Renewal History
http://www.projectrenewal.org/history/

[17]Buisa, Gary. "Gloom Service! Thugs bring fear back to 42nd St.," *New York Post*, Dec. 4, 2011.Online. [accessed August 19, 2020], http://nypost.com/2011/12/04/gloom-service-thugs-bring-fear-back-to-42nd-st/

[18] Roy, Zac. *Historic Midtown Supportive Housing Gets $15 Million Renovation*. Online, 2018 [accessed August 19, 2020], https://patch.com/new-york/new-york-city/historic-midtown-supportive-housing-gets-15-million-renovation

Stephen Boyd, who stars in *Ben Hur*. He is single and 29, but where does that get me? Full of dreams to hide in when there is nobody around I can confide in.

At least, the hotel has an elevator.

Part of my parents' cost-cutting for this holiday is eating breakfast and dinner at the cafeteria-style restaurant on Eight Street, a short walk from the hotel. We push open two large glass doors and enter a steel emporium—steel tables, counters, pillars, commercial fridges, ovens, and food warmers. The white walls provide the only contrast to this shiny grey atmosphere—unless you are lucky enough to get one of the few window seats. Twice a day, Mom, Daddy and I line up at the counter for cereal, toast, eggs, meat and potatoes, and puddings, all served bare-bones style. The food tastes somewhere between greasy spoon and middle-class, but it is a fair trade, so we can afford to visit some of the touristy places.

We walk along the Avenue of the Americas. In the 1960s a couple of landmark buildings sprang up along this street—the CBS building and the Hilton Hotel. However, it is the building that this Avenue backs onto that catches our attention—the Rockefeller Center. Mom, Daddy and I see a matinee there. We sit somewhere in the middle of the audience and watch the Rockettes kick up their legs and dance around the stage in their glittering gold and yellow costumes.

From our hotel, we walk to Times Square, a jangle of vehicular and pedestrian traffic converging. At night, the lights present a kaleidoscope zipping through the dark. We rush by some of the not-so-respectable places; but I sneak a hurried look into doorways. Curiosity leaves this scaredy-cat gawking with wonder, but also feeling like a stranger in a strange land.

We seem to be hitting attractions within walking distance. Mom, who leads me around on Toronto transit trips, refuses to set a toe down in New York's trains.

"They're dirty," she says. "You wouldn't want to go down there, Sharon." She frowns.

I conjure up pictures of dank, dark subway tunnels with smelly, filth-ridden subway cars overpopulated with unfriendly people. In hindsight, she was probably scared of the trains and this fear transferred to me.

We don't take a New York bus either, although I don't know why. They are cheaper than the taxis. We travel by cab to the Empire State Building on Fifth Ave. between 33rd and 34th streets. Today you can go up to the Observatory on the 102th floor, but in 1960, the top Observatory is on the 86th floor. The lobby downstairs resembles a kingdom of gold walls and ceiling, but what I remember most is a crowded room with people milling towards the elevators. I hang onto Mom's hand as she, Daddy, and I follow everyone towards the express elevators. Once inside, I hold my fears and my breath tight inside as the elevator zooms up to the 86th. We make it safely and stroll out to the observation deck. Despite the hot August day, outside on the small promenade the weather seems cooler. But it doesn't cool down the turmoil inside me. I am still trying to keep my heart from crashing into my stomach because we are slowly making our way to the exterior ledges. Peering at the wide, flat cement barrier with black railing on top, I take a timid look out at the sky. Mom seems to have no qualms; she is already at the ledge and gazing out. Daddy is beside her.

"Come on, Sharon," Mom says. "Have a look."

I gulp. Behind me and to my right and left the sounds of other sightseers moving galvanize me out of my stupor.

I tiptoe forward as if to say, "If this doesn't work out, I didn't really do it." The cement ledge is at shoulder-level. Swallowing, I peek through the railings; then force my eyes to look down.

It is dizzying but also incredible to see the cars and people below—like dolls and toy cars zooming through the maze of streets and buildings. The Empire State Building is the tallest building, and I have accomplished something by reaching the 86th and looking without fainting. Mom hauls out her quaint 1920s binoculars, and we take turns staring down below. The people and cars have increased to TV-picture size. When we use one of the telescope contraptions inside the rails, the people and cars become normal size.

We return to the elevator. I hold my breath; my eardrums go pop-pop, and my heart seems to sky-dive to my stomach. But we make it to the bottom, body parts intact.

The next day we take the boat tour to Staten Island—cruising on the Hudson River past the tall buildings and then away from them. The slow-moving trip turns slower as we near Staten Island. The Statue of Liberty looms closer, and when we are parallel to the island, I imagine reaching out and touching the statue. But don't. We don't even disembark from the boat—it just continues around Staten Island and heads back to Manhattan.

Then we pack, check out, and board the overnight CPR train for Toronto.

As the taxi pulls into the driveway of 139, it feels as if I am entering both strangeness and familiarity. The house appears the same, yet different. Daddy puts the key in the front door, opens it, and we go inside. It smells musty and closed up, but I inhale its hominess like a relaxing drug. My eyes absorb the dark wood doors in the hallway, and their gum board-framed doorways are like old friends.

"Albert, we need to turn the water back on," I hear Mom say, as if from a distance.

I start walking through the house until reaching the other end—my room.

"Better open some windows to let in some air." Mom is right behind me and I move to the side of the bed so she can get to the window. "There. That should freshen up the place soon. I'll open my suitcase and bring your clean clothes in so you can put them away."

When she leaves the room I go to the window, look out into the sunlight shining on the green grass, the snowball tree on one side, Mom's red roses trailing the archway on the other, and the hedge leading to the back garden. And sigh, glad to be back home. I forget that home is a four-letter word. It even begins with the same letter as that other h-word, that place of fire down below.

Hell, however, stays away for a bit when school resumes in September. This grade seven year has many revelations for me and will become the first spike in my future creative calling.

The class is split into one row of grade eight students and four rows of grade sevens. I sit three seats from the front in the middle row. Of all my grade school years, this one is perhaps the best. The Bully is no longer here, and Leslie and I are becoming close friends. We walk partway home from school together, twice a day—for lunch and after school. En route we stop at her cousin Wally's jewellery store. We check out the jewellery, but mostly we chatter *at* him. No idea what we talked about; I just followed Leslie's lead in trying to get Wally's goat.

Back in class I don't seem to have a problem with the mixed grades. I find it odd that Shawn, the son of Mrs. Jones the teacher is in this class. However, Mrs. Jones opens doors, literally and figuratively for me. She expands my reading base and shows how reading can provide an entertaining haven when bad things happen in your real world.— Mrs. Jones also lights the spark that begins my interest and ability in writing. And I learn a lesson on the value of friendship, something lacking with The Bully.

Despite Mrs. Jones' students being 12 and 13, every day after lunch, we sit quietly at our desks while she reads another chapter of the novel *The Robbers of Ravenhurst*. I don't know how much is due to her smooth gravelly voice which seems to suit the plot, or the plot itself, but we are captivated. Nobody acts up—no whines of boredom, no doing something else. We all sit spellbound and listen.

And when the new S. Walter Stewart Library Branch opens nearby in newer and larger quarters, it gives me another surprise—Mom and Daddy are now reading regularly. Both obtain library cards and borrow books. Occasionally, I walk to the library with Mom or Daddy.

My reading also leads me to express myself in writing. Mrs. Jones seems to have the same idea, too, because that fall she has us all enter a writing contest sponsored by the Toronto District Knights of Columbus. We have to write an essay, although I have no idea now what I wrote then.

My friend, Leslie, also Italian, speaks English well, but is not a writer. After everyone has submitted essays, Leslie and I are walking home.

"My friend, Josie, who's 13, wrote mine," she says after we exit Wally's jewellery store.

I don't know what to say.

"Don't tell anyone," Leslie says.

A few weeks later, Mrs. Jones announces the winners. My essay came in second and "Leslie's" came in first.

Do I rat on her and lose one of my few friends? She cheated. She didn't write it. I could be first.

She's your friend. And like you, she doesn't have many friends.
She'll dump you. And you won't want to go into Wally's anymore.
But she cheated. I wrote my essay myself. She didn't.
Maybe I could slip Mrs. Jones an anonymous note.
Leslie will know it was you. She won't want to be your friend.
But I wrote mine myself and she didn't write hers. She came in first with her fake entry and I came in second with my real one? Is that fair?

Over and over in my mind, the pros and cons teeter and totter. I would rather be on an actual teeter-totter than have to deal with this. And I hate the teeter-totter in the park. Which one of Mother's Rules of Honesty can I use? Rule Number 2, Rat the truth about somebody and you will be rewarded, only half applies—I would win the prize but lose a friend.

I finally decide that Rule Number 3—lie by omission—will work the best. I keep my mouth shut. Leslie wins the cash prize; we both get to go to the Knights of Columbus District dinner with our parents. Mommy and Daddy are proud of my accomplishment—my coming in second; I don't tell them about Leslie's big cheat.

And I keep Leslie as a friend—at least for the rest of grade school. When I go to high school, she doesn't follow. I think she attends a public junior high school, or maybe Grade 8 is the end of her formal schooling.

It is a lesson based on the axiom that friends come and go. The Bully was the first instance, but here the waters become too murky to swim through to the other side. Was she friend or foe or both?

Meantime, back on the family front—my godmother and Joe Prince, the farmer from down the road, are engaged. Their wedding is November 30, and for once Mom isn't nixing Daddy and I going because it is winter. After all, it is her baby sister getting married.

This time, at least Daddy can remain in the church for the whole wedding—unlike what happened at my godmother's first wedding to Uncle Stanley. As she and Uncle Stanley began their wedding vows, infant me decided to drown out the main event with the big howl. Daddy had to take me outside that time.

"I missed the wedding," Daddy says when telling me the story a few years later. He never mentions the reception afterwards. I don't get the impression he holds it against me.

But for some reason, my godmother and Joe decide to throw the reception in the house they plan to live in—the same house my godmother shared with Uncle Stanley. I can't understand why they don't hold it somewhere else. What about a hotel?

Perhaps because small town hotels in the early 1960s still had the image of dingy, cheap, somewhere women and children should avoid like hell. These hotels still wore the sexist signs of "Men's Entrance" and "Ladies Entrance," as if going in separately stamped you with a spot of respectability—at least for keeping your distance. Inside was all beer, booze, smoke, and come-ons. Not exactly prime wedding reception locations. No wonder the newlyweds opted for the farmhouse and turned the back kitchen into a dance hall.

The slick slide of the fiddle skips across the room, and my new Uncle Joe whirls his bride across the impromptu dance floor a few feet from the curtain which usually hid the chamber pots in the back corner during the winter. They've been removed temporarily. The reception spills over into the main kitchen, where we grab food, huddle and talk around the oil-burning stove. Detroit Brenda, seven years older than my almost 12, sits on a chair near the oil stove. She is slim, now with dyed red hair and a cool attitude. Brenda has collected all the young men around her as she cracks jokes in her Michigan accent. I watch silently from a few feet away. Despite my wishes, I will never come close to being like her, although we do share something similar—our height, with me only one inch behind.

For now, I sit solitary, invisible in my primary and secondary skins of shyness, unaware of one big reality in life, one that never obviously stood out in any of Mom's Rules of Honesty.

The reality is that time moves along and we must move with it or at least acknowledge the inevitable changes. Daddy puts some of it in perspective.

"Joe's okay, but he's not as friendly as Stanley. Stanley always brought you a beer, made you feel welcome."

14: Don't Look Down—Ever

Life is like a piano... what you get out of it depends on how you play it.
—Anonymous

Daddy begins vomiting soon after spring's arrival. I can hear him heaving through the bathroom door. Mother tries everything from toast to tomato soup, but nothing stays down. We draw no comfort from each other, she, the fussing worried wife, and me, the terrified daughter who crawls back inside my pea shell, trying to pull it shut after me. It remains ajar and provides no protection for a 12-year-old girl.

Then Daddy gets recurring headaches that escalate into one big throbbing hurt at the top of his head. It must be torture to bend over the toilet bowl to puke out his guts while his head drums to the same painful beat. He becomes weaker and spends most of his time in bed. Fear fills my mind, body and soul. When I look at Mom, the same fear shows in her eyes. However, she tries to keep a brave face and looks after Daddy. I feel helpless.

Our family doctor sends him to the hospital, this time St. Michael's.

The cancer has spread to his brain.

In those bad old days, when cancer treatment wobbles in its infancy and has only two prongs—slice or burn, the doctor chooses the fire of radiation to try to kill the cancer cells. Daily, Daddy is wheeled into the treatment room and blasted for 20 minutes with volts of radiation straight into his brain. Clumps of hair fall out, and his head resembles an abstract quilt with the white batting sticking out.

Aunt Gretchen now joins the litany of worriers hovering around Daddy as he continues to vomit and endure the headaches. She brings her dumpy flowered housedresses, straight black hair, black oxfords, and bricks of blue cheese that stink up our fridge and would probably kill Daddy if he were home and could keep anything down. Every time I open the fridge my nose cringes at its sour smell. I don't remember Aunt Gretchen ever setting foot in the hospital, but she rules the home front. She commandeers the cooking and cleaning up, supposedly a blessing for mother and me. After dinner, her hands wash dishes while her mouth spews diatribes on the evils of fluoridation, which was not yet in Toronto's drinking water. But she keeps it together for us on the home front.

One day Mom again corrals me in the kitchen.

"Sharon, I have something to tell you," she begins, as we stand, facing each other. This isn't sit-down business. "Your father's cancer doesn't look good."

"Is he going to live?"

"I don't know."

Our hug does not reassure.

Gretchen's answer is to pray. I still hold onto religion then, so take part in our impromptu female trinity circle saying the rosary, as if strumming the circle of beads and muttering praises and pleas—the hallmark Our Fathers and Hail Marys of the Catholic faith—will make my father whole and keep him alive.

St. Michael's Hospital radiates a friendlier air than Western, maybe because the chief guardian angel resides there. St. Mike must have listened to our prayers, because one day when mother and I walk into his room, Daddy smiles at us.

"I ate a cheese sandwich and it stayed down," he says. In that moment, there seems to be some hope.

Soon after, he returns home and Aunt Gretchen departs. I should feel great relief. However, somewhere deep inside me, those early seeds of doubt have begun to germinate. Is Daddy cured for good? I was betrayed once with lies, and although now, Mom Is telling the truth, I am feeling raw. Instinctively I take measures to thicken my pea shell even more…whether I realize it or not at the time.

One of those measures is to expand my teaching abilities from Math to music.

I am pushing 13 and decide I can teach Mom, now in her mid-50s, to play the piano. Maybe I figure five years of learning Bach, Beethoven and Chopin on my pink roxatone piano provides sufficient credentials to instruct. Now that Daddy is back home and back to work, Mom and I are left with the aftermath of his life/death ordeal. Maybe we can use music to heal, even to survive during this supposed return to normal routine. Or perhaps it is a diversion before the inevitable.

So there we sit, Mom and I, side by side on the piano bench. A mirror on the panel above the keyboard reflects our fingers, perched to perform.

"A Car Eats Gas," I say to Mom as I point to the white keys—A, C, E, G—straddling the middle of the keyboard. "That's middle C," I add. I'm following the methods of my own piano teacher, Miss Garlick.

Every Saturday morning at 10 a.m., I still walk the four-and-a-half blocks to private lessons in Miss Garlick's basement studio. Despite her name, she exudes sweetness and competence when her fingers fly along the pianos—her black upright or the baby grand. The only pink in Miss Garlick is her middle-aged puffy cheeks, which with her short grey hair, give her the appearance of everybody's grandmother.

"One, two, three, play it again," Miss Garlick says, as I try to stretch my tiny hands across eight keys, two black keys in between for a sharp or a flat. In the background, the metronome tick-ticks an even beat, as if ticking away the time left for Daddy.

"One, two, three, play it again," I tell Julia. Wearing my teacher hat precludes calling her "Mom." On the cover of *The Conservatoire Music Writing Pad*, Mom has written her name, Julia Langevin, and her address. She doesn't write anything inside.

But in the music books from Miss Garlick, two different sets of handwriting appear—one scrawls directions for "Sharon" and the other for "Julia." In our first piano book, *Michael Aaron Piano Course Grade One*, Miss Garlick writes, "Keep EYES up on music. 1. Repeat 3x names as you play.

2. Play and say counts 3x." Beside Miss Garlick's "Do not look down and play slowly at first," I add, "Count evenly." On another page I seem to give "Julia" a choice, with "Try if you want," but two pages later, with the exercise on "New Positions of the Left Hand," I cross out my name, and add, "Julia, do not look down."

If *I* look down, I might see the blacks and whites that life should dish out. Straight evil or straight good, no slimy wavering grey to leave me see-sawing in unknown places. Stuck firmly in this unknown, like a fly to flypaper, is Daddy's cancer. Maybe if I hit the correct black and white keys while *not* looking down I might marry the straightforward with the uncertainty and come up with a healthy future for Daddy. But I have an inkling that this is just another lie. So, Mom and I busy ourselves in our piano lessons and piano duets. Because, when we sit together on the piano bench, we are sheltered in our own little world of sharing, creating and learning. Solidarity in two. No need to consider what Daddy thinks when he comes home from work and hears us pounding the piano keys. It also hides my differing and confused attitude towards him. Instead of his physical presence filling me with relief, every step he takes, every word he speaks in the house, seems to drive me away from him.

Like an unacknowledged lifeline, Mom and I cling closer together as we continue our discordant piano routine. If we focus on our musical partnership, maybe the music spilling out into the house will touch Daddy and magically march any leftover cancer away.

On another page of Michael Aaron's piano instructions, under the "Music Hour" composition, I become a schoolmarm who can't spell. "Julia, It's not staccato; play more like a run, only not too fast or two slow," I scribble. Already I'm starting to take the middle road, but I'm wavering with a "play what's there" to the obtuse, "Julia, you must come in on the first note of each measure as soon as you say four on the measure before," to the polite, "Julia, please try not to look at the keys."

Try not to look ahead at what might happen tomorrow, next week, next year, or the worry might kill you. Mom and I could tie for first prize as

Worrywart for Eternity, forever driving our brains through gymnastics about what *could* happen.

And something does happen Christmas Day, when we again spend Christmas with Daddy's family—Aunt Marion, Uncle Monty, cousins Felicity, Sarah, and Nina, and Grandma. They are now living in a bungalow in the north end of Toronto. Mom, Daddy, and I have already been up there for a summer barbecue.

That Christmas visit seems to flip everything over on its backside. It is winter and it is cold outside and cold inside.

Daddy has a little too much to drink before dinner, during dinner, and after dinner. Our visit is on the heels of this second cancer storm and maybe he is feeling sorry for himself. Or maybe Uncle Monty is getting on his nerves and making him feel small. Daddy is thin and stretches to only a few inches over five feet. Uncle Monty is 6 feet 2 inches, heavy set, gregarious and loud. In hindsight, while Mom didn't particularly like Aunt Marion, I think Daddy cowered before Uncle Monty.

The dinner, my cousins, that visit, are all forgotten, like a dream extinguished by the morning alarm clock. Until it is time to leave. Then, I am standing alone in their living room and staring at the fireplace. The lights are dimmed, and not even the fireplace can warm the stone cold mantle around it. I shiver inwardly.

"Albert, I'll drive you, Julia, and Sharon." Uncle Monty's voice reverberates throughout the room.

Even that appears strange. Uncle Monty doesn't drive us anywhere. But it is late; it is dark, and it is cold. We bundle up in coats and hats and trail out to Uncle Monty's car, a sedan of unremembered colour and style beyond it having four doors. Mom and Uncle Monty help Daddy into the passenger seat, then she and I climb in the back. Daddy is talking gibberish and Mom's face wears a worried scowl.

Uncle Monty starts the car and we are off. It doesn't feel the same as my godfather driving us home from their place near Bolton. The only common denominator is the dark sky outside. Driving with my godfather at the wheel always gives me enough comfort to curl up against Mom. In between sporadic short naps, I would raise my head and stare out the window at the bungalows nodding by in west Toronto. The view is foreign, but familiar.

Not so in this car with Uncle Monty at the wheel. He isn't a reckless driver—he is driving slower than my godfather. Maybe because there is a drunk on board. Maybe I am ashamed of Daddy. I have seen him drinking before, but never like this. The air inside the car hovers like an electrical storm ready to pounce somewhere but the destination is unclear.

We soon find out where. Uncle Monty pulls the car over to the side on Yonge Street near the city limits. Are we going to have to get on the bus, then the subway, then the streetcar, then the bus? It seems like a long way home. Why isn't Uncle Monty driving us back all the way like my godfather does?

"I'll get you a cab from here," Uncle Monty says, as he steps out of the car.

The cab drops us off in our driveway. Mom leads Daddy in like he's injured his leg or his head. I trail behind, scared. What will Daddy do? He is not my Daddy. It is like some stranger has taken over his mind and body.

Mom must be thinking the same. After she puts Daddy's coat and hat away, she helps him into their bedroom. I remain standing in the living room, my feet fused to the grey and burgundy area carpet, my eyes staring straight ahead at the mirror over the mantle. A few minutes later I hear Mom's footsteps.

"I'm bringing your glasses in here for safekeeping overnight, Albert," she says. She cuts through the dining room to the living room, strides over to the mantle, folds Daddy's glasses and places them bare on the mantle top.

I am still staring at that damn mirror.

The rest goes blank. But in the morning, Daddy appears to be fine. And we return to our version of normal until the next storm.

15: Tales from the Grade Eight Crib

Education has for its object the formation of character.
—**Herbert Spencer,** English philosopher (1820—1903)

Grade 8 is my year of transition from elementary to high school. Nothing is exactly like the other grade school years. Tom, his eight siblings, and parents moved out of the house behind me. But someone returns—Mother St. Helen, my nemesis from the axes and x's fiasco of Grade 2. Now she is our history teacher, but it's her other position—principal at Holy Cross School—that is more extensive.

And my biggest menace.

She is not our homeroom teacher, but she might as well be because of the grip she has on our class. Another nun, the sweet Mother St. Therese, is the official head of our class. She arranges our seating based on our class standing; the one with the highest marks and highest overall average gets the prize seat—by the door. Nora, Robert and I play musical chairs; I think we switch a few times, but I keep the door prize.

Besides the obvious, open the door when someone knocks, I have other duties. Every morning after Mother St. Therese does roll call, she hands me the attendance sheet to deliver to Mother St. Helen. If that were all, I might have learned to handle it. But no, Mother St. Helen decides that whoever is smart enough to sit by the back door is also smart enough to collect the attendance sheets from the other nine classrooms in the building—I am spared the portables. The teachers are supposed to hang the sheets on the door handle outside their classroom but their compliance is 50-50.

After Mother St. Therese hands me the Grade 8 attendance sheet, I exit the classroom. Taking a deep breath, I cross the hallway for the Grade

7 class. Good, the sheet dangles from the door. I grab it and move on to the Grade 6 class. Empty door knob. I hesitate and peek through the door's glass window. The class still appears engrossed in morning prayers. Do I knock? What will I say? I don't want to intrude. Maybe I should collect from the other classroom first. Maybe I can get the teacher's attention. One of the students near the back turns around and stares at me. I jump back.

Dear God, what should I do? I look around as if someone, perhaps my guardian angel, will come by to help me. But it's only me. I scurry across to the last classroom on the floor and grab the sheet from the door handle. Then I return to the negligent class, take a deep breath, lift my hand and knock. The student who previously stared at me answers.

"Can I have the attendance sheet, please? Mother St. Helen wants it." I wave the collected sheets at her and shake my lips into a reluctant smile.

She gets the teacher, who then stomps in her no-nonsense shoes to the door.

"I haven't filled it out yet. Can you come back later?"

I mumble something about Mother St. Helen wanting them before 9.30 a.m. and she says, "All right, I'll do it now."

She closes the door, leaving me standing there, holding the sheets to my chest as if for protection. I hear footsteps coming up the front stairs. Great. I pretend I'm studying the sheets just before I knock. It had better not be the principal. It's the school nurse heading for her office up the steps at the front end of the top floor. She smiles at me and continues on. The classroom door opens, and the teacher shoves the sheet at me.

"Thank you," I say and dash down the stairs.

I get more of the same on the main floor, but surprisingly the kindergarten class and Mr. Bolt's Grade 5 in the basement have their sheets hanging outside. I grab them and run upstairs to the principal's office. I'm hoping to leave the sheets in Mother's In Tray and skedaddle back to class.

"Thank you, Sharon," she says from behind her desk. "Sharon, I have something I'd like you to do."

My heart flip-flops into my stomach. My mouth goes dry and silent. I force myself to look at her as she stands up and grabs a stack of papers.

"I want you to run some of these off on the mimeograph machine upstairs. Come with me. I'll show you how it works."

She charges out of her office, along the corridor and up the stairs. She is like a stubborn bull with a purpose and I am the reluctant matador who must catch, not only her, but catch on to her commands and obey them.

The mimeograph machine is in the lay teachers' lunchroom, up the stairs at the other end of the top floor. No other teacher is present, something I will soon regret. Mother places a pile of blank paper in a tray and gives me instructions.

"Slide the paper in the tray here, like this." Then she picks up a carbon-backed sheet with letters cut into it and wraps it around part of the machine. "...the cylinder. Then you do this. Then you do that. Next you do..." She clasps a handle and the machine, no the cylinder, goes round and round and round...

It is all a confusing buzz inside my head. I'll never remember anything. Sheets are whizzing out the one end, and a heavy inky odour permeates the air. I begin to sway.

"There are three sets of tests and information sheets. So I want you to staple the pages of each set together, like this." She places one set of sheets together, slides them under a small black device, presses down on its top, and after a "thump" sound, pulls out the three sheets attached at the corner. "All right, Sharon. I'll let you finish. You can bring them down to my office." She strides out of the room.

I stare at the machine, which is still running off the copies. It clatters away and I don't know whether to press my hands to my ears or to my nose. So, I just stand still and pray.

Dear God, what am I going to do? Please help me.

Finally, I inch towards the printed sheets and put my eyes closer to them. They are the purple-inked sheets we get for our lessons and tests. I notice these sheets are for Grade 5. I pile up one set and slide the top left corner under the stapler, then press down. The sheets remain loose. I press harder and the stapler seems to stick to the papers. I move my hands away and start viewing them from all angles.

"Please, God, help me," I say out loud. I yank at the stapler and it comes away. Three staples, two of them in, and one bent every which way, join the papers together. I decide to try another set. This one gets stapled with one staple, so I continue with the rest.

Then there are the other two sets to copy. But don't I have to remove that inky sheet with the cuts in it from the machine? I tentatively place my hands on the sheet and try to roll it out. It rips. I yank my hands away. Purple spots are scattered on my palms.

What am I going to do? I want to run home but I can't hide the truth—I have to fess up. I wobble out the door, down the stairs and into the principal's office.

Mother is scribbling at her desk and doesn't appear to see me. I open my mouth but only dry fetid air pours out. Swallowing saliva, I stare at her. She looks up.

"Have you finished?" she asks.

"I got the first ones done, but I can't get the inky sheet out of the machine."

She leaps out of her seat and tears out of the office. Her billowing habit creates an evil wind blowing no good my way, but like the condemned murderer heading for the noose, I have to follow. She's already charging up the stairs when I turn out into the halls.

"Stupid, stupid, you are stupid," she says, as I walk into the mimeograph room. "You do it like this."

I step back as if standing on the gallows. And wish I were.

Mother St. Helen sometimes sends me shopping for bread and milk at the convenience store down the street. Although I'm used to collecting a few groceries for Mom, when Mother asks me, I spiral into worry overdrive. Am I getting the right loaf of bread? Is this the price she said it would cost?

I always manage to pick up the right loaf of bread but also pick up a lifetime worrying habit. True, its constant thump and ricocheting in my mind originated with the mommy gene. The other "Mother," the nun principal, played the part of supplying the bad environment.

However, before I exit Grade 8, I have the chance to show Mother St. Helen that I am not always Stupid Sharon. Whether she likes it or not, this nun inadvertently generates a positive experience for me when she turns teaching history over to the class.

Each pupil has to teach a lesson. We can pick our topic, as long as it is Canadian history. It also gives Mom and me another chance to collaborate in a teaching scenario.

I become caught up in this preoccupation with instructing. My lesson will tell the story about how each province entered Confederation and the plan is to make it more interesting than a history book. Needed are maps, drawings and background history of the history. As she usually does with my school projects, Mom digs in and accumulates some of the research materials, a habit she picked up when I needed information about other countries for school projects. In those pre-Internet days, Mom visited consulates in downtown Toronto as well as travel agencies. In Grade 6, she ordered the whole collection of the World Book Encyclopedia, from a door-to-door salesman. But World Book was no scam—it had detailed coloured maps and detailed text. I use its information as part of the background for my Confederation lesson.

After I put the whole lesson together, Mom and I do several dry runs.

I prop up my maps on the dining room table. Mom stands at the other end in the living room, and I start my spiel. We also do the dry run in the kitchen, where I go through the whole lesson, using my illustrated props and pointing with her long dressmaking ruler. She doesn't tell me to talk slower or speak up; she listens, nods, and smiles. When finished, she doesn't need to say anything. I *know* I have done a good job and pleased her.

My day in class as history teacher arrives. Mother St. Helen calls on me and I cart my maps to the front, support them along the blackboard, and start, from the first provinces into Confederation and tell tales about the "fathers" behind them. I weave an interesting story that keeps the class and Mother St. Helen mesmerized. I don't falter as I lecture, ask questions, comment on the replies, and answer questions posed by some of the other students. It is as if I am transported into another world where I tell true stories, and everyone hangs onto my every word. I don't recall the class clapping when I finish, but can feel it in the air that they learned history without yawning.

Teaching history gives me a warm happy feeling inside. Perhaps, Mother St. Helen will now give me some respect. But I am too naïve to know that a leopard never changes its spots –no matter what her guise. When the last day of grade school arrives, this truth hits me harder than the baseball bat we used in our school baseball games.

Mother St. Helen comes to our class to hand out our report cards. She sits at Mother St. Therese's desk in the front while the latter takes a seat at the back of the classroom. This principal doesn't just give out the report cards, she calls our names in ascending order of standing, and we have to walk in pride or shame to the front. I'm hoping to stand first again, and I do. However, Mother has the last words about me for the whole class when she compares me to another student.

"Now, Harry may not be as intelligent as Sharon," she says, "but he has something she lacks—common sense."

Heads turn towards me. My face heats up and I want to crawl into my desk and make it disappear, preferably over the rainbow. I can't wait to leave Grade 8 and go to high school, especially as this isn't my only humiliation in June 1962.

Just before finishing Grade 8 at Holy Cross, I play at a recital staged by Miss Garlick for her students to plunk their chords and arpeggios on the piano. This is not my first recital.

At eight, I breezed through my initial Miss Garlick concert. We had to play without the music sheets. I don't remember the next few concerts, but I remember this last one, ironically, in the same time frame I was teaching

Mom to play the piano and the year after Daddy's hospital stay. The concert takes place in the Heliconian Club in Toronto's Yorkville.

While waiting to perform, fourth from the last, I hang around two old school friends and Kathy, another Miss Garlick student. We venture out the club's side door into the pre-Hippie Yorkville, with its Beat poetry and music, bearded young men and long-haired women sitting, smoking and drinking outside cafes. After returning to the Heliconian Club's back room, my number comes up.

Miss Garlick introduces me. Mom and Daddy sit near the front of the audience. Daddy dressed up in his best pin-stripe suit and post-radiation hairstyle of white hair tufts doesn't detract from my resolve to play it right. Besides, as Julia's teacher, I have to set an example.

My pièce de résistance, Debussy's *Clair de lune* (Miss Garlick's choice), provides a challenge. My sweaty palms carry the sheet music as I step through the doorway and onto the stage. A quick glance at the hushed audience sends my heart galloping; I reduce everyone to a blur and avoid looking at my parents while sitting down at the sleek black baby grand. After arranging the music, putting fingertips to keys, taking several deep breaths, it is time to begin. If I keep hitting the right blacks and whites, maybe Daddy's life will continue. My only choice is to slide right through, especially the muddle of chords on page five. Don't look up. Don't look down. Don't look anywhere. Just keep going.

On page five, I strike a wrong chord. My hands freeze a few inches above the keys. The audience breathes in silent anticipation, but it sounds like a roar inside my head. I don't dare look up at Daddy. He must be so disappointed in his little girl. So I stay still, my face hot for the hellfire I deserve.

Miss Garlick sticks her head out from the backroom doorway and yells, "Turn the page." Her voice reverberates across the front of the audience, to the street entrance, back through the audience, and over to me.

I turn the page. My hands unfreeze and I fake my way through the rest. When finished, I stand up, in a fog with no memory of anyone clapping

(They probably did, out of kindness). I have embarrassed myself and failed my mom. What kind of a teacher messes up playing at her concert? I never want to play the piano again.

But I will continue piano lessons with Miss Garlick until I turn 15 when bopping along to the top 40 at high school and church youth club dances, and listening to the Beatles with my friends, beat pounding chords to the tick-tock of the metronome. Mom learns how to play simple tunes on the piano. Soon after I start high school, she will no longer have time for piano lessons.

16: The Summer Between

Female adolescence is—universally—an emotionally and psychologically intense period.
—**Caitlin Flanagan**, Writer

Before high school I have to make it through summer, including a holiday at my godmother's and Uncle Joe's in July. But I am 13 ½ now and feel differently towards Daddy. Something seems out of whack. We arrive late at night, and after tomato soup and crackers, we settle into our designated bedroom—the family living room. It's not so much that Daddy nearly died from cancer, although looking back that probably had something to do with it. At the very least, Daddy's cancer scare makes it harder to deal with the family logistics, particularly the sleeping quarters.

In the stark bright morning light, I wake up to Daddy's snoring. I look down at Mom. She is still sleeping (and also snoring) on the trundle. I don't want to get up with him in the room. I don't want to get dressed with him in the room. I hide under the covers. Maybe it will all go away and I'll be home in my own room. There I have taken to keeping my bedroom door closed, especially when Daddy walks by in the hall to his and Mom's room. Here, at my godmother's, we don't even have hospital curtains. Soon Mom wakes up, gets dressed and exits the room.

"Get up," my mind tries to persuade me. I look across the room at Daddy, still snoring.

I can't do this. Somehow I want Daddy to be moved out of the room. Finally, I get up, and in between surreptitious stares over at him (still sleeping, still snoring), I manage to get dressed under the blankets. Then I bolt out of the room.

In the kitchen, Mom and her sister are chatting; I have no idea about what, because I am trying to work up the nerve to tell Mom I can't sleep in the same room with Daddy. I am too young, too naïve, and too stupid to know why.

"Mom," I finally say, when my godmother leaves the kitchen, "I have to um, talk to you about um, something."

"Yes."

"It's about um, Daddy."

"Yes, what about Daddy?"

"I um, I can't um, sleep in the room with him."

She must understand and she probably has some conversations with her sister. Because that night I get to sleep upstairs in the girls' bedroom, in the same bed as the two oldest girls. It's a small room, with two beds, the largest pushed up against the wall. I'm on the outside so don't feel hemmed in, except when Linda or Margaret sit up, climb over me, step out of bed, pull the chamber pot out from under the bed, and use it. The rest of the time the three of us chatter into the night. I don't get much sleep, but feel more independent and comfortable.

August shows up too soon and brings with it a hacking cough. I cough my insides out and can't eat because the chewed food blends in with the mucous in my throat, and out they both spew.

Mom calls the doctor. I'm too old for a pediatrician, so she has switched me to the family doctor whom she and Daddy see—an old bachelor in his late 40s who won't get married until I am in my 20s. He's very friendly and respectful, but I am shy around a male doctor.

He prescribes a sweet red cough syrup, which doesn't seems to dispel the cough. The thick mucous in the throat gags me in between meals. Bed becomes my new abode, except for visits to the bathroom and one hour allowed up to watch TV. I drag a blanket and my vomit pan—the plastic bathtub that came with my doll, Darlene—and sit on the designed-to-split chesterfield in the bright living room. When TV time is up, I collect my belongings and return to bed in a room darkened by drawn blinds and drapes. I gaze at these blinds and imagine they contain people sketched in their cream-coloured creases. I create stories; then my eyes move to the drapes and the flowered design takes on the head of a lady who must talk to a little girl who won't listen. But I do—to my transistor radio, hearing the Everly Brothers sing *Crying in the Rain*. It seems to suit my situation. Daddy brings in the daily newspaper for me and pulls back the drapes. He doesn't say a word and doesn't look at me. I don't know if he is frightened for me because I am sick. The situation is reversed from last summer, but I don't catch on, just stare at him as he leaves the room. Then I pick up the newspaper and read that Marilyn Monroe committed suicide.

I still read books, but my selection is way off the mystery and teen angst marks. Instead, I am tackling the whole Book of Genesis in a white-covered Bible with coloured pictures inside. I am well into Exodus when my friends Marie, Jan and Dorothy drop in for a visit.

The three cluster together at the bottom end corner of my bed, near the door. Easy exit. They stare at me as if I am an enigma. I stare back, afraid to open my mouth because of what might fly out. The bathtub is under the bed and it better stay there. I am so scared they will see me vomit and too immature to consider they may also be afraid. Maybe they think I am going to die and if they move too close it will rub off on them. Marie sets her face into a smile and nods. Then Jan opens her mouth.

"How are you doing?" she asks.

The ice is somewhat broken and they tell me what they are up to this month. I shake my head. What can I say? I'm plugging through the Bible? Dorothy would get a kick out of that.

I feel the familiar tickle, then the heave in my throat. No. Not now. Wait until they leave. I start coughing, low and slow at first, but it builds up. Mom rushes into the room, hauls the bathtub out from under the bed, and places it in front of me.

"Oh, your throw-up bowl," Marie says.

After I am through, the three of them decide they'd better leave. They don't make another visit. I don't get outside the house until late August. Maybe that's why in high school I will make such a big deal of sitting out in the sun on the veranda or in the backyard, sunning myself while reading a book when I'm supposed to be doing homework.

17: Tales from the High School Bunker

True terror is to wake up one morning and discover that your high school class is running the country

—Kurt Vonnegut, Jr.

Labour Day looms near. I continue hacking, but the doctor deems the cough spells are far enough apart for me to start high school. I have graduated from doll's bathtub to facial tissue and handkerchief, but don't feel comfortable doing the cough-and spit-up routine in public.

Mom and I have to go in to Notre Dame a few weeks early to buy school uniforms and books. We take three buses—three minutes on the first two and 15 on the latter. I should feel excited, but terror rips through me.

Notre Dame is still one small building. When we walk into the tiny "sale" room I feel smothered. Books and clothes are piled on tables set up in a U with two Notre Dame nuns standing behind them. They are the "sisters" of the ones at Holy Cross, but what did I expect in a school with the name Notre Dame? Mom purchases the navy blue skirt, vest, four white blouses with long sleeves and collars, and a maroon clip-on tie. Then we get to the stocking display.

I seem to have stepped into The *Sound of Music*, but hitting all the sour notes. One of the nuns stares at me staring at the stockings. *Black lisle hose and black nylon seamed stockings. Oh holy yeck. It can't get any worse.*

It does, when I find out what we have to wear on our feet—black oxfords. Old lady shoes. When I dress for school, I turn into Granny Sharon. Perhaps that's why I don't remember the actual first day of Grade 9. However, many of the following days snap into place, including Picture

Day. Mom trims and washes my brown hair, which has more of a mind than I do. It appears layered with one clump sticking out. Red lipstick (the nuns' one concession to make-up) adorns my lips and a sprinkling of acne highlights my chin.

The bus rides to and from school are different from that first day with Mom. I have to leave earlier, and it is a trip in extremes—the nearly empty Broadview bus with only Karen and me in our frumpy uniforms, hauling our books in schoolbags, to the three-stop ride on the O'Connor bus, wedged in with the work crowd. We are too early for the students at East York Collegiate across the street, so no one needs to get off except Karen and me.

"Keep moving," the driver urges everyone, but it is too tight to squeeze back towards the rear exit. We try hogging the front area so we can leave at Mortimer. I am worried we will miss our stop. As the bus crawls nearer, I struggle to lean around a man reading a newspaper so I can pull the rope over the window to announce our intended departure.

The bus jerks to a stop and Karen and I continue swaying by the end of the side seats. I am panicking, pushing and pressing my way between arms, backs and scowling faces.

"Excuse me; I have to get off," I say. "Sorry," as my books whack someone's back.

Someone else steps on my right foot, and even the thick Grannies can't cushion the hurt. My breathing picks up speed, as Karen and I finally reach the top of the exit stairs. But the people are already piling in.

"Excuse me, we have to get off," I say.

With a final thrust forward we make it out and breathe sweet fresh air. It never occurs to us to walk the three blocks bus number two covers. I suppose we figure the driver on the third bus wouldn't honour our transfers, but he wouldn't see us walking; we usually have to stand around and wait for him to arrive.

Bus number three isn't full yet, so we find seats. When the bus gets to Woodbine, the fellow I like from the boys high school near Notre Dame gets on. Every day I see him, I want to speak. I have found out his name from a girlfriend. He is a year older than me and he looks like the actor, Chad Everett. One day, he actually takes the empty seat beside me. It's now or never, Sharon, I tell myself. I guess it is never.

When we arrive at Main and Danforth, the students from Scarborough board the bus. Most of them have to stand and they tower over me. I peek between arms and heads for my friends in class—Pam and Freddie. Sometimes I let them put their books on my lap. I know from my three-stop experience the difficulty of balancing books on a moving bus. At least, we are all headed to the same stop.

On the trip home, often I have to stand and, unless my friends are there, I feel like an outcast. While the buzz of conversation goes around me, I merely clutch my books, nod, and look around. The guy I like is also standing, near the front of the bus. Why should he notice me, with my mousey hair, messy face and frumpy body encased in a shiny dark blue skirt, black stockings with seams and old lady shoes?

Those old-lady shoes and seamed stockings probably helped give the appearance of maturity, as our Grade 9 teacher saddles Pam and I with some extra responsibility. Nothing like the master-slave thing I had with Mother St. Helen in Grade 8. Mother St. Christine, our home-room teacher, is just the opposite of St. Helen. Sure, she is strict, but she is funny and takes a lighthearted attitude to some things, like the big teased hairdo of Arlene who sits one up from me in class. When Arlene leans to one side, Mother St. Christine says, "Oh, I thought that was a bird's nest."

But when it comes to smoking and skipping classes, Mother St. Christine is on the holy warpath. She assigns Pam and me as "buddies" to Clare, who has a habit of sneaking out between class to somewhere behind the school for a smoke.

"Your assignment," Mother says to Pam and me "is to make sure she gets from one class to another without any detours."

Pam and I are on Clare's back but have no clue how we will keep her on the classroom track. When she strides off course after Math class, Pam and I hurry up to her.

"We'll walk with you to the next class," Pam says to Clare.

"Oh, I have to go to the bathroom."

Clare has a sly look on her face which blends in well with the foundation makeup and lip gloss. At least, she doesn't tease her hair. Maybe she should, as it hangs down in straight brown shreds to the top of her neck.

Pam and I look at each other and we both shrug. Mother didn't mention anything about bathroom patrol.

"Fine," I say.

Clare goes off and pushes open the bathroom door. We don't follow her. I figure it would be invading her privacy. So we head for class. Of course Clare is late arriving.

"Well, Clare, I see you have had another adventure," Mother says. "You are late and so have a detention after school."

Clare shrugs. She has that sly smirk on her face again, and, as she passes by my desk, a whiff of cigarette smoke drifts past. While looking at her face, I realize she is very pale and it is not from getting a detention. This is her normal colour—foundation makeup or not. She is like someone trying for ghosthood and, perhaps, the cigarettes are all that keep her going.

Sometimes, after school, I don't make it to the bus with my friends. I start out. We're strolling along Kingston Road; they're chatting, and I'm silent outside but my mind dashes north, south, east, west and every spot in between.

Did I lock my locker? I can't remember and can't picture locking it. What if I forgot? I can't remember turning the dial in the lock. I hope I locked it.

My footsteps stop abruptly. I apply Mom's Rule No. 3 in honesty—lie by omission.

"I forgot my history text, so I have to go back," I say.

"Okay," Pam says. "See you tomorrow."

Juggling my books, I swing around, and speed-stroll back to Notre Dame, yank the door open to the now-built new school extension, dart inside and upstairs to the corridor near my classroom. I do not stop until standing in front of my locker. Then I let out my breath, drop books on the floor, and stare at the locker.

Of course, it is locked. Feeling relieved and stupid, I glance in one direction—the other three are the window, the end wall, and the lockers. No one is coming at me from that fourth direction. Just in case a classmate or a teacher materializes, I actually unlock the locker, open it and grab a notebook and shove it into my school bag. Then I slam the door. While sliding in the lock and turning the dial, I repeat in my head, *I am locking my locker*.

It doesn't stop me from taking a couple of glimpses back while walking away. The locker door does not swing open.

But I don't want to return to the five months we spent in the portables while the contractors continued to finish the extension. The portables did not contain lockers, only wooden shelves, spread under the window along one side of the portable. We each had one cubicle to stuff in wet boots, hats, and school bags. We crammed our books into our desks or carted them around with us when the ink wells froze in winter because the oil heater at the front wouldn't kick on. We were nomads on a mission—find an empty room where we could commiserate with God for our religion class. Usually we ended up in the cafeteria.

The cafeteria exudes that hot water radiator smell in winter. When we wander in during the first period, the sun bestows a bright cover on the room, and it almost seems homey. We can't get anything to eat then and must suffer our growling stomachs until the early lunch.

At 11.30 a.m. we again file into the cafeteria, this time with brown bags in one hand, purse in the other or slung over our shoulder. The sun has disappeared, and the room now wraps its dull grey atmosphere around us and attempts to suck the life out of everyone while we try to refuel with what our moms packed in our lunch bags. As I sit at our designated class table with Nora, Milly, Martha, Freddie, Pam and Carol, I remain quiet and listen to their chatter. I haul out my usual—peanut butter and jelly or jam sandwiches, a thermos of milk (I can now open it myself), and an apple, skin intact. Afterwards, my stomach feels a little sour, like something didn't go down right. Or maybe it is the surround sound in our portion of the table. When Freddie and Carol get going, the air fills up with more than old radiator smell as Freddie tips over to the snarky and superior edge, and Carol becomes the voice of standing-her-ground assertiveness. Sometimes, they do the opposite. Freddie aligns her seating with Nora, Milly, and Martha. That leaves me with Carol and Pam. Pam is my friend. But so are the others, particularly Nora, who's been with me in the same classroom since kindergarten. Sometimes she will sit with Pam and me. I'm treading into crowded territory and, if I lean either way, something might collide. I'm not on anybody's side. I just want to fit in with everybody.

I also want those rip-roaring comedy sketches Pam and I do in the girls' washroom in Grade 11. We make sure only the two of us are present. It is not our friends we poke fun at—it is the teachers. One of us acts, and the other has to guess the teacher's name.

Pam scrunches up her face to make it look dried up like old Pruneface, an old lay teacher. Then she lowers her voice.

"Girls, mumble… mumble… you…must,"

"Oh, it's Mumbles, Mother Mumbles," I say.

Pam's face jumps into her wide smile and we giggle like we're hiding something. I take a quick look at the bathroom door, but it remains closed. Pam covers her mouth. Now, it's my turn. I back up almost to the door, lower my head, scowl and charge forward.

"No, No, No," I say as I stop a few inches from Pam.

"Mother St. Gregory," she says, as we both shake, rattle and almost roll with laughter. We are never caught.

Despite the bathroom shenanigans, I tried to remain a good girl in high school. My browner status decreased a little in Grades 9 and 10, because the competition increased. But I kept most of my high marks until grade 11—

then they began to freefall downhill. I blamed the Board of Education shoving the new math at us, but much had to do with swirling teenage hormones and dealing with Daddy's cancer.

When I moved into my teens, I started a practice common to adolescents—hogging bathroom time. I would stand on the bathtub ledge, stare into the mirror at my face, call myself ugly and fat, and then visualize myself far away and with different parents. Daddy began using the laundry tub downstairs to brush his teeth, his mug and toothbrush resting on the inside shelf of the two-by-four wall of the old coal storage room. Although the basement had the finished rec room by then, it contained no bathroom.

Some rejections are subtler. Every fall, the all-girls high school I attend holds a father-daughter dance. In Grade 9, Daddy and I attend, me in my homemade outfit labelled *Mother*, and him in his pin-striped suit and white tufted hairdo.

"I'll show you how to dance," Daddy says. "You just follow my lead; move your left foot, then your right." He steers me around the high school gym. We keep bumping into other father-daughter couples, and every time he says, "Pardon," I am mortified. Daddy is trying, but dancing with him seems awkward, out of sync. He stands only two inches taller than me, but his patched white hair makes him look old and odd.

His illnesses could read like a medical litany as Mom and I discover in my second year of high school, when Daddy starts vomiting again.

One night, I hear a loud thump in my parents' bedroom.

"Sharon, come quick. Sharon." Mother's voice pounds through the wall.

I jump out of bed and charge into their room. Daddy lies sprawled out on the floor at the end of their bed. Mom says he was headed for the bathroom, but after a few steps, passed out.

Mother is frantic. I've never seen her so out of control. She bends over Daddy, shouting something about "ambulance," "doctor" and "hospital." Her panic must give me some incentive, because I run into the dining room and phone the doctor's office. Of course, I get the answering service.

In the 1960s, no 911 service exists; Toronto has a mishmash of private ambulances for emergencies. Finally I connect with an ambulance service. During the interminable wait, mother throws on a housedress and "old lady" laced shoes. I pull on my school uniform; thinking I'll go from hospital to school. Now, I have vague pictures in my mind of the two of us trying to lift Daddy back onto the bed, but I don't remember if we succeeded.

The ambulance finally arrives amid flashing lights and off-the wall sirens, like an introduction to a nightclub from hell, with the main event a jarring Rhapsody in C-minor. The neighbours are probably standing, around gawking in their housecoats and pajamas, stunned from being rudely awakened to sirens. But Mom and I are oblivious.

The hospital admits Daddy right away. Mom and I spend the rest of the night sitting in those uncomfortable and unpleasant chairs in a small room, no doubt set aside for families to weep and worry. The newspapers and magazines don't capture our interest. Mom and I alternate from staring at the cream ceiling to the beige walls to staring at each other. Occasionally, Mom mutters words of encouragement, but as her tiredness increases, her hope seems to decrease.

After that horrendous night at the hospital, with no answers about Daddy's illness, I return to school a day later, only to be called to the principal's office.

The call comes over the PA. I stumble from my desk in our classroom in the new building and try not to feel all eyes staring at me. I haven't done anything wrong, so it must be about Daddy. With my heart pounding and my mind racing faster than my feet are taking me down the stairs, I whisper, "Please God, let Daddy be okay." Despite distancing myself from him, I don't want him to die.

My head feels hot as I wind down to a slower, but still unsteady walk into the old school and then down the hall to the principal's office. I can see her, an old nun, tiny in stature, sitting at her desk. Her wrinkled face is set in its usual grimace. She is on the phone and when she sees me, she puts the receiver down on the desk.

"Your mother is calling about your father."

"Yes, Mother," I manage to reply. My voice feels and tastes like chalk dust.

I remember talking to Mom on a phone but it seems like it is a pay phone on the wall, which is silly in a principal's office. More likely, Mother Principal handed me her phone and I talked briefly to Mom.

"It's not cancer," Mom says. "The doctors found a duodenal ulcer and they are going to remove it tomorrow morning."

So I take a few days off school—a breather for me, and for Daddy, or so it would seem in retrospect. Daddy's younger sister, Aunt Marion, joins us in the wait at the hospital. The doctors remove the ulcer, and, as he recuperates, he suffers a mild heart attack. I hang around, in his room, in his presence and willingly listen to him talk about missing his retirement party at work. That doesn't seem right to me and it saddens me that he won't experience this milestone. However, he doesn't appear sad or rueful; he sounds almost cheerful. Is he putting on a brave front to try to win back his daughter? Neither of us speaks about it directly, but I continue to visit him after school and on the weekend, until he is released from the hospital. However, when he returns home, I revert to avoidance mode. Daddy's tummy and heart heal physically, but emotionally he is left stifled and silent. Alone inside his body, mind, and soul.

18: Boys, Beatles, and the 15 to 20 Club

True love is like a pair of socks: you've gotta have two and they're gotta match.
—**Author Unknown**

I am now lost with Daddy, so I turn to my friends. Not to confide; it is more like a complete absorption into what they are doing, with me tagging along.

Four of us—Nora, Jo, Anna and I—decide we don't want to line up in the school auditorium for our student TTC tickets. After school, we take the Mortimer bus to the Danforth and switch to the streetcar—this was just before the Bloor Danforth subway line opened in 1966. I sit by the window, open on this warmish spring day, letting the breeze blow on my face. We are able to wear our burgundy school jackets, probably the only appealing part of our school uniform. With these three friends who have also gone to Holy Cross, I don't feel so lost. We exit the streetcar near Coxwell. We have business to attend to and maybe those uniforms show it. But we spoil it all by dashing in between the cars from the streetcar platform to the sidewalk. I'm at the rear, looking both ways and wishing we had gone the half block to the lights.

We hit the sidewalk running, panting and relieved that nothing metal hit us. We slow to a business-like walk. Jo pushes open the front door of the old TTC building where we purchase our student tickets, then exit for another run through traffic—this time to the other side of the Danforth. After all, cola and fries, the teenage diet, wait for us in the Bus Terminal Restaurant. We order a round of the drink and huge plates of greasy French fries drowning in thick gravy. A late afternoon snack at 4 p.m., while we dissect some of our homework and then move on to more important stuff.

"St. Mike's has a dance this Saturday night," Nora says. "My brother told me."

"Are you going?" I ask.

"Probably. What about you?"

"I'll have to ask my mother. But if she says yes, I'd like to go. What time does it start?"

"Eight o'clock." Nora turns to Jo. "Are you coming?"

"Probably."

Anna won't come. Her parents won't let her.

"I'll let you know, tomorrow," I say.

We finish our snack and then head home. As I sit on the O'Connor bus, I try to concoct a story why I am late. Drama club won't work, as I quit that after the first semester in Grade 9—Mom didn't like me coming home alone in the dark after rehearsal. I like drama and was sorry to give it up even though my only on-stage part was one of the crowd visiting the baby Jesus in the stable. I wore a long shift and had a white sheet wrapped around my head. Nora said she recognized me by my nose.

But I need to get past mother by more than just a nose. Which of her rules of honesty would fit? I open the front door and enter 139. I smell stew beef cooking and hear the pressure cooker, puffing away on the stove. But the kitchen is empty. I poke my head into the living room. No Mom. I walk in and continue to the dining room where I plunk my bag of homework down on the table besides Mom's sewing machine.

My mind races but the thoughts don't form into coherent reasons for my late arrival.

"Mom," I say. It is almost a whimper. "I'm home."

I hear a door in the back, then footsteps, and I swing around. Mom stands in the doorway. She's holding part of a dress-in-the-works.

"Sharon, I need you to try this on so I can measure for the zipper," she says.

At supper the three of us sit around the table. Daddy is not saying much and I'm not looking at him much. I can't seem to eat with him sitting there. My mind fastens on my latest fantasy, where I'm at the St. Mike's dance, dancing with a guy I've just met and like. That reminds me I have to ask Mom if I can go.

"Sharon, you're not eating. How come you're not hungry?" Mom's voice cuts through my brain fog.

I look down at my plate and realize I'm swishing my potatoes, cream corn, and stewed beef around on the plate as if turning them into mush. Then I also realize the practical reason for no appetite—my big fat snack.

"Oh, just thinking of my homework." I put some of the mush-in-progress onto my fork, move it into my mouth and start chewing.

"Do you have a lot of homework?"

"Some. Well, for tonight."

"What do you have?"

"Math, a bit of History, and some English."

"Well, hurry up and finish your supper, so you can get at it."

"Hmm. Mom?"

"Yes."

"Nora wants to know if I can go with her to the dance at St. Michael's High School. It's on Saturday night."

"Well, I don't know. You have homework to do."

"It's the weekend, and I can do my homework Saturday and Sunday afternoon."

I glance up at her, then down at my plate, and put another forkful of potatoes and beef onto my fork and resume eating.

"Well, all right, but make sure you get your homework done first. And make sure you go with Nora and come back with her."

"Jo is going, too, so there will be the three of us. And Nora's big brother goes to St. Mike's, so..."

Mother frowns. I didn't mean big brother *that* way, but as sort of a protection for his younger sister and her friends, although Nora never said he was going to the dance.

"Hmm. Okay. Now finish your dinner and do your homework. No TV until you're finished it." She turns to Daddy. "Albert, do you want a cup of tea?"

"Hmm. Yes," he says.

I struggle to clean my plate, and out of the corner of my eye see Daddy stand up, grab his cup of tea, turn around, and walk silently to his and Mom's bedroom. When I hear the door close, relief and guilt dance a tango inside my head. I really don't know what to do with my daddy. His illnesses have disconnected him from me. He is now this elderly man, with those tufts of white hair, leftovers from the radiation treatments when I was 12. He seems older than my Grandpa Charlie when he stayed with us to heal from his operation. I bonded with Grandpa, and also as a little girl, with Daddy, but can't seem to do it anymore. It's as if when he first went into the hospital and had half a lung removed, the operation also removed any essence of the king protecting his princess, especially when I finally found out it was cancer. Deep down I know he won't be around for much longer and I just don't want to deal with any of it. So, I leave everything to Mom. I re-enter my teenage daydreams of boys in my actual world, and those actors and rock stars who are unattainable, especially the British invasion of pop stars.

None of us, even the practical Nora, are immune. Beatles, Rolling Stones, Dave Clark 5— we swoon over some or all of them. But we can't agree on who is the most talented. I argue with Abbey in grade 10 class in the portable (when Mother St. Irena is out of the room) about who sings better—the Beatles or the Rolling Stones. Abbey is a diehard Stones fan.

"They're too loud," I say.

"No, they are better than the Beatles," Abbey says. She is tall and thin and seems to wear authority in the Notre Dame uniform. I think it's because she seldom smiles.

"But Paul is so cute," I say about my favourite Beatle.

"George is my favourite," Nora says. "He is different."

"Paul," I repeat. "But I also like John."

John is the radical of the bunch and maybe that's why he appeals to me, the straight-laced Catholic schoolgirl. Religion will play a part with the Beatles and one of my school friends, but surprisingly Mom will be on my side.

Not the first year the Beatles come to Toronto. Mother refuses to line up outside Maple Leaf Gardens for tickets on a school day, and so I miss seeing their performance. I hog the radio, TV and newspapers for reports and photos, and almost have my ears up to the lips of Martha, the only classmate who gets tickets. On Labour Day, she screams her way through the first Toronto Beatles' concert. The next day at school, Martha can barely talk above a whisper. But she and I pass our poetry about the Beatles back and forth during class until Mother St. Irena catches us and snatches the poem. It feels like she is stealing my heart. I hate being caught and singled out. But when one of my Beatle poems that I submit to the local rock station is read on air, I make sure everyone knows. Maybe the writer in me is peeking out—not just in the actual writing, but in the actual blowing my own horn.

The second year the Beatles come to Toronto, Maple Leaf Gardens places a large ad in the *Toronto Daily Star*. You can order tickets by mail. Three of my girlfriends and I get parental permission to go, and Mom places the ticket order.

Ruth, Nora, Jo and I are the lucky four. We have seats on the side, up a little in the bleachers, but near the front. When the Fab Four, as the Beatles were nick-named, run onstage and begin performing, we can see them, although not their features up close. However, everyone is screaming and we have to hear the lyrics and music from memory. I jump up and down and rock in my seat, perhaps to verify that I am really here.

When it's over, we are sad and happy. We seem to glide down the stairs and out the doors of Maple Leaf Gardens as if in a movie turned down to slow motion. Our ears have ventured across the street, or maybe they remain back inside the Gardens, leaving behind only this muted roar. When one of us speaks, the rest of us stare at her face, watching the ups, downs, and sideways motions of her lips. Once back home, my ears revert to normal.

Normal was also boys in real life. However, I was late to enter the dating scene. What did I expect with no big sister to pave the way, and Mom playing an ultra-conservative hand? And I didn't exactly hang around with a fast crowd. But when my Catholic friends started going to the 15 to 20 Club dances Sunday nights in the basement of Holy Cross Church, I had to go.

However, there was a problem—I was two months shy of my 15th birthday. So I had to do the Big Convince—twice.

First, there was the priest who ran it –fortunately not Father M. but Father T., and I needed his permission to join the club early. I like to think I approached him after Mass on Sunday and just asked. Or maybe I had Nora do it for me. I don't think I asked Mom to do it because she was Number Two in the Big Convince.

"It's not really dating." I slide it in between forkfuls of rhubarb and strawberry pie as I face Mom at the end of the kitchen table. I had to wait until Daddy left the table. I'm not comfortable getting into this dance thing in front of him. I don't know how much of my discomfort is because of his cancer and how much because he's more like a grandfather in age than he is my father. So, Daddy fills his cup with tea and takes it into the bedroom to drink alone, and I'm waiting for Mom to answer my question.

She pauses, fork midway to her mouth.

"Father T. will be there to supervise." I lean forward. "He says I can join now instead of waiting until December when I turn 15, because now is the beginning of the season. Nora, Jo, and Pauline go. I can meet them there. And we go to Benediction in the church first." I stop to suck in air.

Mom slides a piece of pie into her mouth and gives it a few chews. I dig my fork into my last pie chunk as if it is my lifeline, but my eyes never leave Mom's face. *Say something* I want to shout. Mom swallows and opens her mouth.

"What time does it finish?" she asks.

"Eleven p.m."

"That's kind of late when you have to go to school the next day."

Silence at my end.

"Hmm," Mom says. "Well, okay, but I'm coming to meet you halfway home afterwards. I suppose we can give it a try, but make sure you meet Nora there."

It's not Nora I plan to meet. When you are shy and can't look a guy in the face without blushing, you need more ammunition than another friend who has never dated, even if she is full of common sense and nothing seems to faze her.

No, I call in the pro.

Marni.

I hung around Marni when we were 11 and she, her brother, and their parents first came to Toronto and to Holy Cross. She was Austrian, but I don't remember if she was born in Toronto. Her parents weren't and they spoke little English. That one summer I was down at her place often while her parents worked. I gathered they lived sparingly because Marni boiled eggs for our lunch. But playtime wasn't with dolls; we were into the adult thing—pretend dating. The guys, of course, were imaginary, but not invisible to our eyes.

By the time we were in 10th grade, Marni had a steady boyfriend, Don, who played guitar in a local teen band. She'd also transferred from Notre Dame all girls' school to the mixed bag of East York Collegiate.

I call her, and she agrees to meet me just outside the front door to the church basement at 8 p.m. I can handle the Benediction alone.

After the service, I park myself outside and try to look as if I belong. I stand straight, put on a smile, but keep pushing my short hair back as if that will turn me into a femme fatale. Guys I knew in grade school pass me by. They seem to have leaped up in size. Some are cute, but I avoid looking at them. What do they see in a mousey browner who stopped growing at 13? I can't help pacing like Daddy sometimes does. My mind jumps like a yo-yo in distress and my heart tangoes with my stomach. This isn't what I mean by dancing.

Where *is* Marni?

I strain my neck beyond the walkway and look up and down Donlands. No Marni in sight. She should be coming from the south. Maybe she's walking along Cosburn. My eyes dart north. No Marni.

Where *is* she? More former classmates and teens I don't know come by. They talk and move in their own little world of confidence. I want to blend in. I want to go home.

Where the hell *is* Marni?

Finally, when my stomach has about devoured my heart, she struts up Donlands. She's wearing a short tight skirt, pump-heeled shoes, model makeup, teased hair, and the know-how of a 25-year-old fashion queen. I stare down at my mom-labelled corduroy jumper, white long-sleeved blouse, and black pumps. I feel like a leftover from a nunnery and wish I was invisible.

"Hi Sharon." Marni smiles. "How are you? Let's go inside."

She leads, with me floating behind as if in a bad dream. Inside, we pay the entry fee.

"Hello," I manage to say to one of the girls at the table.

Once on the other side, we head for the Ladies. Marni chats away while I try to stop feeling strange. Perusing my face in the mirror doesn't help. I take out comb and lipstick from my purse and try to make myself look a little more than just human.

Then we're heading out into the hall—the main area. Marni stays with me for a bit; then she starts to make the rounds. I see Nora and Pauline, so I join them. Except for couples going steady, the girls sit on one side and the boys on the other. Then Randy, the club DJ, gets the turntable rolling, a Top 40 charter rockets through the room, and the dance ritual begins.

I try not to be a wallflower as boys I know and boys I don't know venture over—at first, just a few brave ones. I smile too hopefully, and when they choose Pauline or some other girl, I wilt into the chair. A pitcher of water poured over my head won't revive me, and I'm wondering whether this is all some mistake. Maybe I should have waited until actually turning

15—as if December will magically turn me into a woman who knows all the answers and can at least carry on a spontaneous conversation.

Then Randy shouts into the mic, "Snowball Dance." One couple starts dancing; when Randy stops the music and yells, "Snowball," the duo splits—the girl for the boys' side of the room and the guy for my side. Eventually I get asked to dance a number of times. I make it through the evening—no dates, but I have fun. And I don't exactly get to walk all the way home alone. Mom is waiting for me at Donlands, south of O'Connor. Fortunately, all my friends go the other way home. I mean, I'm nearly 15 and they don't need to know that I have to hang onto my mother's skirts.

This scenario continues for the next five months. My dance card doesn't get full, and for Ladies Choices I sometimes ask guys I knew in grade school to dance. I sense they do so out of politeness. I have nothing much to say to them, but make a new friend—the 19-year-old brother of a former classmate. There are no heartbeat feelings between us, but I'm comfortable with him, and we can converse.

My first date is someone from outside the parish, a 15-year-old Italian guy, Joe, I have never met before. He's not particularly tall and handsome, but his hair is dark and he asks me to dance. As they say, we get talking.

"Do you want to go to a movie?" he asks.

Yes. Yes. Gee, what do I say? Should I ask Mom first?

"Okay."

We spend the rest of the evening dancing and deciding what movie, what night, what time. Then he wants to walk me home.

Great. Maybe Mom will show up late.

Of course, I have no nerve, so I say, "Yes."

After putting on boots, coats, and hats (I do the latter), we stroll up Donlands, past the bungalows. While we talk—I have no idea about what, probably about where I live as he thinks he's taking me there—I dart looks in front. No Mom yet. Are we early?

We cross Plains Road, walk by the jewellery store and past the Donlands Cinema. I crank my head over towards Joe, then down, supposedly to watch my footing in the snow. I sneak a look up the street, and there she is.

Mom is heading our way, and I want to duck into the Donlands Restaurant with Joe but am too chicken. But wait. Mom is doing her diplomatic thing. *She* pulls into a doorway, Hurst's Drugstore, I think. Joe and I keep on talking and walking. I feel Mom's eyes on us.

When we stop for the lights at O'Connor, I turn to Joe.

"I can walk home the rest of the way myself," I say.

"You sure?" Joe asks.

"Yeah. It's just up there." I point to my right.

"Okay. I'll call you sometime during the week."

"Okay. Good night."

"Good night."

Fortunately, he doesn't kiss me. Mom catches up with me. Now, I'm in for it.

"I didn't want to embarrass you so I stepped into the doorway," she says.

Of course, I tell her about Joe and the planned date—*my first date. I'm jumping for joy—inside.* When I look back on it, I know I was excited for that reason, not about Joe. Just as well. As first dates go, mine had its own bizarre twist.

I don't remember what I wore for that date or even caring what I looked like. My mind is all curled up in dating protocol. The concern is not about kissing on the first date (I'm not Marni), but with bus tickets.

I cannot get it out of my head that Joe may expect me to pay the bus fare. It is a date and the guy is supposed to pay, I keep reminding myself. But this is my first date and the worry clouds are storming around inside my head. When they part, I see Joe and me getting on the bus, him putting one bus ticket into the box, and me standing stunned as if I'm not really there. I don't call Marni and ask her advice—somehow I know she will think I'm stupid and naïve. However, I make sure there are bus tickets in my purse.

Saturday arrives and so does Joe—with his best friend, another guy. I am furious. Why didn't he tell me he was bringing a friend? I could have brought one of my friends, not Marni, but maybe Ruth. Joe's friend is really the third wheel, so why do I feel like the extra?

It never dawns on me then that maybe Joe too is nervous. Butterflies galloping through the stomach can make you do strange things—or in my case, think strange things. I needn't have worried about bus tickets, although I do ask Joe if he has a spare—maybe his friend's presence boosts my nerve to do so. Joe plunks a bus ticket in the fare box for me, and the three of us file to the back.

I have no idea what movie we see or what theatre we attend. Don't you usually remember the movie on your first date? I guess our threesome date doesn't qualify as more than an embarrassing oddity.

There is a vague picture in my mind of the three of us sitting in the dark theatre, gobbling popcorn as we watch the screen. Joe sits beside me, but I'm not sure if the friend is on my other side or Joe's. Afterwards the two of them take me home by bus and that's it—first and last date with Joe. Not your high-tension romance.

I continue to go to the 15 to 20 Club but don't meet any memorable guys there and certainly don't pick up any more dating leads. Nora and I move on to other Catholic churches that hold youth club dances. At Holy Name, I meet Frannie who soon becomes my cohort in crime to hit the youth club dances and con guys into dancing and dating.

Frannie is a year and a half younger than me and she has skipped a school grade. Although old enough for these dances, she is not old enough to work. Eventually she will get herself into a pickle with her part-time jobs and two SIN cards.

The two of us have a routine. We descend on either the Holy Name Friday night dances or St. Monica's dances. Sundays, we alternate between Holy Cross and Canadian Martyrs. We meet at Holy Name hall, but for St. Monica's she hurries up on the Yonge subway after her stint working at Kresge's downtown. We rendezvous at the Eglinton Subway Station where we head into the washroom to ready ourselves for St. Monica's. During the hair combing and lipstick applying, we catch up on each other's personal news. I discover that Frannie lives a very different life than me— she seems to be alone and doesn't get along with her mother.

"I want to leave home when I finish high school," she says. "So I work part-time."

We stop once at her place on the way to a dance because she has to pick something up. She won't let me in because of this mother-daughter dispute, so I wait outside.

I mined a few fellows as dates, mostly from Holy Name. I could sure attract the eccentrics, but hanging on to them was another matter. It was usually my fault—I just let them go. Sometimes, I became bored with them; sometimes, no spark erupted between us, and sometimes the spark seemed one-sided. I think I missed having an older sister to confide in. Certainly Mom wasn't the best person for this role, although we had a few conversations about how not to get pregnant.

And then I met Gary.

We connect at the Holy Name dance. He is 17 to my 16. Our combined dating experience wouldn't even rate an unlit candle to Marni's experiences. Gary stands tall, skinny, with medium brown hair and acne. On one of our dates we go skating together at the outdoor rink at Dieppe Park. The actual skating scenario is a blur, but considering my penchant for clutching the skate guards in my hands when skating solo, I probably had some inner turmoil about whether to ditch the guards and hang onto Gary or keep the guards and let Gary slide his arm around mine. A real dilemma for a people-pleasing personality with yellow stripes down her back. I probably took the happy medium—skate guards in one hand and entangling my other arm with Gary's. I don't recall falling on my face or on any other part of my anatomy.

After the skate, we walk the 15 minutes to my place. Daddy isn't home, but Mom is.

We're sitting in the living room, Gary and I on the chesterfield which splits in the middle and Mom over on her pink easy chair by the bookcase of *World Book Encyclopaedias*. Mom has made us hot chocolate, and while we sip and slurp, she's asking a few questions.

"Where do you go to school, Gary?"

"Central Tech."

"Oh, that's a few blocks south of where my sister-in-law and her family used to live on Markham," Mom says. "Do you live near there?"

"The lady I live with…" Gary says.

My face turns crimson. I know it isn't what it sounds like, but I wish he didn't put it like that. Mrs. Wheeler or whatever the woman's name is will do.

"…she's my foster mother. There are five other kids there," Gary continues.

I look up from my hot chocolate and smile. Mom has a placid almost blank expression on her face as she nods. She's asking Gary something about what he's studying in school.

"Shop," he says.

And so it continues with our dating—we go to movies, some of the dances, but when we start hugging and kissing, I feel the horns of the moral dilemma growing inside my head.

What if it gets out of hand?

How will I stop him?

What if I get pregnant?

And the question I dare not ask anyone because they'll think I'm dense– can I get pregnant if we do such-and-such?

I have learned well the teachings of the nuns, the priests, and the Catechism about what good girls didn't dare do or they'd commit a mortal sin and be labelled "fast" or worse.

Like Rita in my Grade 9 class. She is tiny, pretty with black hair and like the three other girls she hangs around with at Notre Dame, she runs wild. The fast foursome are always huddled in hushed conversation about their latest dates.

One day, Rita is collecting all her books and other things—she is clearing out for good. "I have a lot of problems with my teeth," she's telling us as she hurries out the door.

Back then I believed her to a point, but I couldn't quite grasp *what* point. Today, I realize that Rita was pregnant.

Subconsciously I know I have to get some answers somewhere. Without an older sister to confide in, it has to be Mom. We've talked about this pregnancy issue before, but she hasn't delved into enough specifics about what is safe. I am swimming in hormonal confusion and I need to reach clear.

Over and over in my mind, I rehearse what I will say to Mom. I swallow hard, walk up to her and just smile. Finally, I ask her.

"Mom, can I talk to you for a minute."

She nods.

"Can I, can I, well, get pregnant if Gary and I...well, if we... if we just like put our arms around each other and we're close and kiss and..."

"Now, Sharon, you remember what I told you before. No, you can't get pregnant just by doing that."

I am not convinced. Like the old Greek men who finger their worry beads, I finger this problem—but in my mind. I am trying to convince myself that it is okay; I will not get pregnant from hugging and kissing. But the problem is that I am afraid Gary and I won't stop at this.

So, I stop seeing Gary. Just like that. We are no longer a couple.

I ignore Gary at the dances, even when he comes up to me and asks me to dance. Once while walking up Bathurst from Bloor Street, I look up and see Gary coming the other way. When we get up close, I turn away and ignore him as if we had never met. I have no clue how to behave, but think I also still like him and have made a mistake dumping him.

By then, he is ignoring me too. As we pass each other, he keeps his mouth closed, and his eyes open on the street ahead. Can I blame him?

I'm creating a pattern. When I call it quits I don't want to see the fellow anymore, anywhere. The *why* is not clear, but maybe it ties in with expectations. When you catch the guy, isn't it supposed to be happily ever after like the fairy tales say? But there is also what the Catholic Church, the nuns, and priests say. And there is what Mom says. And there is what I say—in my head—worrying about what might happen. If we had kept on seeing each other, Gary might have left me, and I couldn't stand that.

I'm already swallowed up in this leaving dilemma with Daddy and his cancer—all the yo-yoing between will he live or will he die? While he struggles to survive, I struggle with probable abandonment. Daddy is the first man in my life and represents an anchor to grab. Going from the over-protected princess to the daughter of a cancer patient feels like the whole floor is crashing under me. So I retreat emotionally from him because deep inside, I sense that he is not long for my world.

Maybe I am carrying this recent change, this rift, into my dating life, feeling I *have* to dance warily with any guy I date because deep down I know that it may not last. Or maybe I am just too stupid to know better. I may not have had a big sister, but in looking back and digging below the surface, more comes to light.

Maybe this caution is some form of inner control. If I can't control what happens to Daddy, and if I can't control what happens with any other man in my life, perhaps I need to step out of this particular picture because the future appears too terrifying. The underlying message from Daddy's cancer seem to be—don't get too close; don't get too involved, and whatever you do, don't get into any real commitment. Because it won't last. The deeper you are, the more you feel, the harder it is to climb back out and get on with your life. Much easier to just coast and try to have fun.

But fun is in short supply. In the fall Nora and I are switching high schools for Grade 12. Nora is just fed up with Notre Dame. With me, it is that, but also Mom, who is worrying about money to pay the bills. With Grade 11, Mom had to start paying an annual tuition fee for the year at Notre Dame. East York Collegiate being a public school, requires no tuition. It also is closer to home and offers more course options, although Nora and I will soon discover this won't apply to us because of our limited course options starting with Grade 10 at Notre Dame. We should have transferred to East York Collegiate in Grade 10, like Marni did. Hindsight is not always better sight.

19: Boys, Girls, and Teachers

Extroverts never understand introverts, and it was like that in school days. I read recently that all of us can be defined in adult life by the way others perceived us in high school.
— **Neil Peart**, Musician

East York Collegiate is a hefty change from a small high school of around 600 girls to a large school with double the population of both genders. So, on the first day, I make sure Nora meets me outside the front door. I can't venture inside alone. It is difficult enough to get on the Broadview bus. When I step off to cross Coxwell instead of rounding the corner for the O'Connor bus, I am almost filled with nostalgia. For what? The push/shove of the crowded bus, and wearing old lady shoes and a shiny uniform? Now I get to wear normal clothes. As I make my way onto the actual school grounds, clusters of chattering, happy girls and boys surround me. I feel my anxiety level rise beyond the top of my head, but no one says anything to me; no one even *looks* at me. I am not here…I am…

"Sharon."

I swivel around. Nora is walking towards me.

"Hi," I say.

I follow her inside the school and we look for the office where we have to pick up our schedules. My feet are almost touching the back of Nora's heels and I am certain the curse, the blessing, whatever it is, of us always being in the same class, will end.

We are in the same class with the same timetable. And our lockers are side by side, but around a bend in the hallway, away from our classroom on the second floor. We have no trouble finding this classroom and step inside to another group of faces, bodies—all chatting away, no doubt catching up on their summer holidays. But there is one fellow we recognize—Rod from

Holy Cross. Rod was actually a year ahead of us so I guess he failed a grade in high school. But we don't mention it when we stride over to him.

"Hi," Nora says. "You went to Holy Cross. I don't know if you remember me but I'm Nora Clarke."

"Hi," I manage to say to Rod. "Sharon Langevin."

He remembers us from the youth dances at the church.

A sweet-looking old lady who reminds me of my Grandmother Lou enters the room. When she opens her mouth, the sugar ferments into bitter no-nonsense.

"Everyone take a seat, please," she says. "I'm Mrs. Term, your homeroom teacher. I will also be teaching you French the beginning of each day in this room. Your schedule will guide you to your other classrooms."

I find out more in our first French class, when I open the French book and see the byline—*Frances Term*. Great. No getting around it. I'm doubly stuck—a French last name *and* the teacher who wrote the book. And I don't come from a French-speaking family. Class, however, begins with PA announcements, then the singing of *Oh Canada*.

"After the announcements every morning, we will read from the Bible," Mrs. Term says, as she passes out small copies of a blue-covered New Testament. "It's the St. James version. Now, if there are any Catholics in here who might take offence, please raise your hands and you won't need to participate."

I look around. Rod has his hand raised. So does Nora and another short girl, pretty, with olive skin. I can't be the only Catholic who reads a Protestant New Testament, so I raise my hand. It feels strange sitting there, an outsider to the only religious practice in this public high school. But no longer do I have to see or suffer from nuns and their religious fervour. Instead we have some men teachers.

One of them is crippled, or, what we now say, has a disability. Thanks to having polio as a child before the vaccine, his legs are in irons and he walks with crutches. It is too bad his essence is so rude and sarcastic, because it is not kind to belittle someone who is crippled. Mom and Daddy never do. Mom just mentions that so-and-so uses crutches because they had polio.

But this Mr. Green who teaches us Latin is a creature in another vein. As we file into our first Latin class, Rod whispers to Nora and me, "He tells dirty jokes." I see this short old man, with grey hair, a reddish face with only a few lines in it, leaning his arms into two crutches. His cold blue eyes stare at each of us as if he is assessing our worth.

Then he slides open his thin mouth and out pours pornography. His rude sexual jokes disgust my Catholic upbringing. Half the class quit after two or three sessions. They have a spare option. Nora and I can't because we drag along our minimal four options from Notre Dame—Math, French, History, and Latin, so we are stuck. To make matters worse, Mr. Green can't teach Latin, and the textbook is from a different series than at Notre Dame. For two days when Mr. Green is off sick, we get the younger, cuter teacher, Mr. Gryphon. I wish for Mr. Green to stay off permanently, but he returns.

The first semester my Latin exam mark tips into a pass but when I add up the individual marks for each question, the total decreases eight points. Several exercises in mental math don't change the bottom line. Thanks to Mom's Rule No. 8 in honesty—tell the truth even when you know it will get you into trouble, because lying or staying silent just doesn't seem right—I *have* to speak up. After class, I sneak up to the front, as if I've committed a crime and clear my throat.

"Mr. Green. I, uh, I think there's something wrong with my mark. It doesn't seem to add up."

He frowns and grabs my exam paper. His eyes scroll down the pages and his lips move as if saying a litany, but he's only whispering numbers.

"You're right," he says, scratching out his correction. "You're an honest woman."

For the moment I feel I've "done good," in honesty, but definitely not in Latin. For the first time I have failed in a subject.

If I think Latin and its teacher hit rock bottom, my math teacher appears to live under a rock, and overturning the big stone is the only way to find this out.

Mr. Crowe stands at the front of the class, a dumpy-figured man in a beige suit. What remains of his black hair slithers its way across the top of his head and adds nothing to a face that seems to have come further from seeing better days than Mr. Green's' face. He prowls his short torso across the front of the room, down the aisles between our desks, and scowls his words at us…not at Nora and me, but at most of our classmates who had the privilege of his presence and instruction the previous year. It doesn't really get to me until I follow his advice—"Anyone having difficulty in Math can come here after classes and I'll give extra help." I figure I better try to sort out the new Math this year.

So here some of us sit, coming for "extra help" and instead getting an extra dose of sarcastic insults shoved at us—except for me. Mr. Crowe always makes sure he names his target. He leaves me alone, but because of my experience with The Bully and the nun in grade school, I feel for these other students, and because of his treatment of them, I quit going for extra Math help. I occasionally ask Nora, but really have trouble understanding this new Math, and it is added to my failure list.

If I thought the men teachers were cruel, I had yet to meet my PT instructor. Miss Dorian twisted and turned Physical Torture into her own version as she bullied us into dancing like fairies, doing the run-jump (in my case run-crash) to and over the wooden "bull" in gymnastics. In archery, she hit her bull's eye with me.

We are lined up to string our bows and then shoot some arrows. Miss Dorian stands tall and slim with short blond hair flat against her skull, face etched in wrinkled hard lines, and mouth needing the bleach more than her hair. She blasts out her instructions.

"First you do… then…" Her voice is low. *Gravel Gertie*.

I am trying to string the bow, but it is heavy and won't bend like she says it should. The string has a better mind of its own than I do. I look up. Miss Dorian is staring at me.

"What is Sharon doing wrong?" She smirks like a gargoyle.

I freeze up.

"Come on. What is Sharon doing wrong?"

Except for Nora, her friend Lillian, Rod, and Terry, I usually feel lost, left out, someone who beamed in from another planet. Not today. All eyes are on me. My face heats up and I can sense its redness. I try to keep back the tears, especially when Miss Dorian strides over to me, grabs my arms, hands and the bow, and takes me through the stringing processes. It is too bad I don't have enough nerve to grab the string and strangle her. But I am still a good Catholic girl and I believe murder is wrong, although I suppose justifiable homicide is permissible.

Somehow, I make it through the rest of the torture without leaving the room. But when we return to the change room (actually the equipment storage room), I figure everyone will laugh and make fun of me. One by one—Susan, first, then the others—come towards me. I know I'm in for it now and try to stop the tears.

"Don't let her bother you," Susan says. "She isn't worth it."

"She's been having an affair with a married teacher here for years," another of the girls says.

Warmth suddenly engulfs me. Although I can still feel the heat of the encounter with Miss Dorian, it has pushed back to a lighter heat. I cry full-fledged now, but 90 per cent of my tears are tears of surprise and gratitude.

This Susan, one of my United Church friends whom I sometimes played dolls with as a little girl, will again be instrumental in connecting me with some of the other girls in our class.

The Beatles are coming to Toronto again, but Nora, Ruth and Jo don't want a repeat concert performance. Nora is now more interested in what's happening with her peers.

This time, Maple Leaf Gardens automatically mails my mother a form to order tickets. My head is still swirling in the fantasy cloud, so I ask Susan, and surprisingly her mother says, "Yes" to her request.

One day, Susan and I are standing on the sidewalk outside East York Collegiate. Some of the popular crowd in our class—Dana, Lou, Maggie—stand right next to us in an open circle talking amongst themselves. I pretend to listen and not listen, and try to think of something relevant to say. Something that will show I am worthy of them. But my lips and voice do the opposite to their actions at last year's Beatles concert.

"Sharon and I are going to see the Beatles," Susan says. "Maple Leaf Gardens mailed her tickets."

The eyes of the popular crowd turn to me.

"Lucky you," Maggie says.

"Fab," says Lou.

Even Dana is smiling at me—she who seems so intimidating, probably because she is tall and heavyset. I murmur a weak "Yes," and smile back. Why can't I say more? I know Maggie and Lou, the twins, from Miss Garlick's piano lessons.

Then John Lennon makes his famous "The Beatles are more popular than Jesus Christ" statement and Susan's mom pulls her permission. Susan returns her ticket to me but it is too close to the performance to get someone else to go, and I'm too shy to ask anyone. It never occurs to me to ask one of the popular crowd. The second ticket gets sent back to Maple Leaf Gardens, and Mom lets me go alone. The new ticket holder is a 13-year-old girl, who after intermission, moves to sit with her brother and his friends in another section. I'm left alone to see, listen, and fantasize. This time, I sit on the same side in the bleachers, but way, way down from the stage. The mop heads appear small and far away but I can hear them singing. I don't scream because my friends aren't around to join me in letting out my emotions.

But John Lennon's statement stuck, and I found myself trying to defend it, mostly in my mind. Looking back, the seeds of discontent with religion may have already been planted inside me, although Lennon's statement wasn't what would make me question the righteousness of religion, in particular the beliefs of the Catholic faith. My own home situation with Daddy having cancer, coupled with the change in society norms coming right up against the religion-by-rote from grade school would take care of that. This time Mom wouldn't stand on my side and no one would be there at 139 to confide in.

***

Despite the minor connections of solidarity with my peers, I still feel like an outcast. Through the school halls, I drag a heavy burden of books, baby fat, and an invisible zipper on my mouth. I lighten my load with the lack of any sense of style or person. During school hours I hang around with Nora, Lillian, and Terry, who is in our class. He also has his locker in that area around the bend, so he and Nora commiserate while the three of us haul books in and out of our lockers. Unlike Notre Dame, we keep everything in a locker—sometimes sharing space with others. I have a locker pal, a transfer student, for all of two months in the fall, until she transfers herself out. I don't have a crush on Terry, but I consider him neutral. A few times I make him guinea pig to test moving past my shyness.

Nora, Lillian and I buy these hot little red candy hearts. We suck and swallow them like they are well, candy. Perhaps it's the cinnamon in them that hikes their temperature a few notches in our mouths. I decide I want to share this treat with Terry.

"Here, try one of these." I hand him a red heart and try to keep a straight face as he swallows it.

"Holy cow," he says. "That's hot."

Another time I get braver. The three of us are all talking—I have no idea about what—but I'm playing around with my locker door,—swinging it back and forth. Terry is standing nearby, and—whack! My locker door collides with his knee.

I am mortified and apologize. Not exactly the way to a fellow's heart, even when you are just practicing.

However, my year at East York Collegiate had something much worse than feeling lost because of my shyness, and trying to cope with strange surroundings and stranger people. Something that began in the summer before I switched high schools and continued into the fall.

Daddy's cancer returned.

20: D is Also for Daddy

Reconciliation is more beautiful than victory.
—Violeta Chamorro

The house dynamics change. Daddy is now retired and struggles to find sense in a house with no one else there. After remaining at home for nearly 16 years, Mom returns to work. I stay away a lot—at school, out with my friends, at dances, and at Beatles' concerts. Even when home, I keep my nose in a book or in the newspaper. The latter plays a part in Daddy's continuing effort to win back his daughter's love and camaraderie. He and mother play "good cop/bad cop" with my reading habits. Mother rules no reading library books or newspapers until I finish my homework, and so she "hides" the newspaper on the downstairs steps. Daddy carries it in and places it on the kitchen table. I read it, but never thank him, never even acknowledge his gesture. Instead, I continue treating him as someone who must be present, but not in the same world as mine. I have curled up inside, far away from the 13-year-old who sat at the piano with her mother, teaching her to play, and deep down, hoping our music would help Daddy heal. Didn't work. So, the family that hides away, stays safe…for a time. The rude awakening always smashes in.

Daddy, however, still wants to work in and around the house.

In the summer, just before switching high schools I am sitting inside, reading an Agatha Christie mystery, when there is pounding on the front door. The mousey-haired nurse from across the street, stands outside. She looks angry and starts scolding.

"Your father passed out when he was cutting the lawn," she says, twisting her plain mouth into a frown. "I helped him up. He's okay now."

Daddy also begins to act vague, like his mind and his body are slowly splitting. Every time he urinates in the bathroom, he misses the toilet bowl. Mother worries that he is going senile. With all this happening, it is no surprise that he lands back in St. Mike's.

This time he is beyond burn and slice. He gets shipped to Riverdale Hospital, storage facility for the unwanted—those people waiting to die. Although Riverdale oozes starched cleanliness, doom filters down its hallways and into each room. Daddy alternates between lying in bed and sitting up. A photograph, taken by a cousin, shows him seated on a chair in the sunroom, wrapped in a red corduroy housecoat that almost makes his pallid face and limbs disappear, but black socks bring his legs into the picture. Under the housecoat he wears a pajama top, opened halfway down his chest. He stares through black-framed glasses, a smile set in place. His right hand grabs his left wrist as if holding on for a life no longer dear. With the Don Jail still functioning next door to Riverdale, his surroundings do not enhance the dignity of living.

But the living must eat. During one of our visits, Mom encourages Daddy to endorse his pension cheque so she can buy food. She sits beside him, like a schoolmarm trying to get a student to form letters in penmanship.

"Albert, just make an *X* here." She guides his hand along the practice sheet of paper.

He stares at her, at the paper, at me. I move my eyes to the pencil in his hand, and Mom's hand covering his.

"Here, try again," Mom says. She bends over him as though trying to breathe life into his cancer-dead brain.

Yes, I am visiting Daddy and continue to do so after school and on weekends after I start at East York Collegiate. Hiding away didn't make him better. However, I have not yet arrived at a place to feel comfortable talking to him beyond saying "Hello Daddy" and the other bland phrases that flow out automatically from our mouths when someone close is dying. Baby steps. He doesn't seem to hear me anyway. He is too far away from his little girl. I am too late.

Mom and I seek sanctuary by pacing the dimly lit hallways, staring at their lime-green walls, as if the more steps we take will tally up the payment for his mortality and bring him back. More likely, we pace to make time. When our feet and thoughts tire, we head for the sunroom, sit, and gaze at nothing in particular.

But the day Daddy dies, I have a revelation.

Mom and I have taken a break from being physically present with Daddy and have gone into the sunroom. We sit in silence absorbing the bright sunlight streaming through the windows and warming the bland green walls. Like magic. Like…but no music is playing there or in my head. Something else is making an entrance inside. A voice. Daddy ? Has he managed to break through and connect? And why now, one year after I stopped making music on the piano? Considering the message, perhaps the music had reached him, but he was waiting until he had something important to say.

"Go into your Daddy's room, *now*, he's dying," the voice says.

Third person. What do I expect when I have shunned Daddy? I turn to Mom.

"We have to go to Daddy. Now!"

We stand and hurry along the hall. When we arrive at his bedside, Daddy is beyond voice, beyond action, beyond thought.

"I'm sorry for the way I treated you," I say in my head. "Goodbye, Daddy."

I'm am sure he hears me as he travels from this life to the next.

Then he is gone. Mom and I are left with a feeling of sad emptiness. So many times we were expecting him to die, but when it really happens, it leaves us dumbstruck. Mom, being the practical person, decides we need to be busy. I guess she is thinking of the funeral because she leads us downtown to Eaton's and Simpsons, but it is not one of our happy shopping trips. We go straight to the ladies department at Eaton's to pick out our mourning dresses.

It is my first adult dress for my first real adult loss—at the age of 16—five years short of being legally adult in 1965. The deaths of my grandparents and uncle pale in the family circle as I come to dead centre. This is my Daddy and I must show him some respect. I choose a black dress, in slim A-line style with long-sleeves ending in a ruffle. A flat matching ruffle hugs the high collar-line. The dress falls below the knees and when I try it on it fits perfectly. If I don't look at my face, I could be mistaken for a tired 41-year-old.

On the streetcar going home, Mom and I stand, clutching our Eaton's bags in one hand and the back of the seats with the other. The silent eyes of this rush-hour crowd dig into my heart until I look up at them. They stare at the streetcar ceiling, the floor, a newspaper; they have no idea what we carry in our bags or what has happened. I have no desire to tell them and continue to clutch and crouch towards the seat as the streetcar winds up Broadview towards the Danforth where we switch to the Broadview bus for home.

There may be only Mom and I left at 139, but by golly the aunts, uncles, and cousins are not going to miss out on paying their respects and disrespects. Some show up at the funeral parlor, where Mom and I have held court for the past few days and evenings. Nora and Jo pay a visit to the parlor, and we sit drinking coffee in the waiting room. The principal and vice principal from East York Collegiate also make the obligatory call at the funeral home. I am sure they don't remember me among the school's many students. But those four are the only ones from school who stop by. When I return to school after taking a week off, I will find that nobody else knew—none of my teachers, and probably only a few classmates.

But the day of Daddy's funeral, Mom and I follow his coffin being carried out to the hearse, and step into a black car to follow behind it to the church. Some of our relatives follow; the rest are already piled into Holy Cross Church for Daddy's funeral, and we continue afterwards for service at another Holy Cross, the cemetery in Thornhill, just north of Toronto. Afterwards, we all troop back and crowd into the living room, dining room, and kitchen at 139. Mom's side of the family scrunches side-by-side with Daddy's —the country bumpkins with the city sophisticates.

Mom delegates me as chief server. I trip over feet, purses, and legs jutting out and touching as I pass around the plates of egg salad, salmon, roast beef sandwiches (white bread with crust removed, of course), pickles, and celery sticks. Mom and her sister, my godmother, look after the beer, coffee, and tea.

"Do you want a sandwich?" I ask my Auntie Clare as the plate wiggles between my 16 and ¾ -year-old fingers.

"Thank you, dear," she replies. "It won't make any difference to these." She points to her very large breasts, her words hidden from everyone but me, thanks to her brother-in-law, my Uncle Monty, trying to carry on a conversation with Aunt Gretchen. Auntie Clare frowns and adds, "I wish I could just cut them off."

The plate wobbles. Does she not remember that it was the chest area where the cancer started in my daddy? Her own brother...

"Well, are you going to pass around the sandwiches, or do you plan to stand there all day?" Uncle Monty asks.

I feel my face turn red but manage to open my mouth.

"Oh." It comes out like a squeak. "Would you like a sandwich?"

"I already said I did. Do you have roast beef? Should be lots of that with all the farmers on your mother's side."

I want to snatch his gray curly hair and yank it, but it is after my daddy's funeral and Uncle Monty is family too, albeit not by blood. So I try to let him be and point to a beef sandwich. He grabs three. I begin to move towards Aunt Gretchen, but Uncle Monty isn't finished yet.

"Being a waitress—that suits you. But you should be more graceful."

I swivel towards Aunt Gretchen, almost sending the plate into the lap of her drab blue and black housedress.

"Have you got any egg there?" She grins showing her yellow teeth. As she leans forward to take a sandwich, her flowered straw hat bobs on her head. "I won't drink water. Toronto water has fluoride in it now and that can kill you."

I stare down at her sensible black oxfords stuck at the end of what little of her legs poke down from her dress. My daddy has just died and so far two relatives have talked about death and dismemberment without any thought for Daddy. Have they no respect?

Somehow I manage to finish the jagged round over feet and purses. I set the plate down on the dining room table, which is pushed against the back wall to make room for more family members to clutter up what is supposed to be home to Daddy, Mom and me. I can't wait until some of them leave and I can at least breathe again. Snatching a couple of sandwiches and pickles, I plunk them on a plate, grab a serviette and sit in a chair by the dining room door.

And so it goes for the rest of the day and into the evening until only the out-of-towners remain. I have had enough of my relatives and head for bed early. Visions of Daddy keep disturbing my entrance to sleep. Him wheeling me along on my bike when I was nine. Daddy yelling at my friends and me because we yanked leaves off his trees to feed our dolls supper. Daddy locking Dorothy and me in the basement for our protection from The Bully and her gang. Daddy rolling those damn cigarettes in the basement. Daddy's mind gone and his body almost there, too.

The din of voices from the kitchen wafts back to my bedroom. From the Polaroid photo my Detroit cousin Laurie takes, and which I won't see until years later, I eventually will guess what went on. Mom, my godmother, and Uncle Joe, sit around the kitchen table, half sprawled over it with beers in hand and empties cluttering the table. Mom stares at something off camera—maybe she sees Daddy or maybe she is looking for him.

Was she already worrying what she would do now that Daddy was no longer around? Her sister, my godmother survived with seven little children after her first husband died, then she remarried. Mom only had me.

Part Five: Off To Work I Go

Sharon's Tool of the Secretarial Trade

Sharon at Toronto Island Weekend off from work

21: Hi Ho and All That Work Jazz

Work is the refuge of people who have nothing better to do.
—Oscar Wilde

"I can go to Shaw Business College for a year." I pout at Mom. "Then I can go out and work."

It is the end of Grade 12 and my report card has arrived in the mail. I passed English, French, Chemistry and History, but flunked Math, Latin and P.T.

The spring before this last year of high school I had made a half-assed attempt to apply for a job at Kresge's and Woolworth's. Frannie got hired at Kresge's, Nora at Ma Bell, and Anna as a dental assistant. But nothing for me. I put the blame squarely on the shoulders of the vest, skirt, seamed stockings and old lady shoes—the Notre Dame School uniform—which I wore for job searches. So, this summer after Grade 12, I don't bother job-hunting and remain the lady of leisure, lounging around on a patio chair and reading.

Summers were for play, but when autumn approached, serious schooling was necessary. I just wanted to choose the school and courses. In Grade 12, despite, or because of the switch to East York Collegiate, I had lost interest in the business of academia—Latin, French, Math, Chemistry, and Physical Torture. After Daddy died, I endured the rest of Grade 12 until its failing end. I wanted to get out in the work world as fast as possible with the easiest obtainable skills I could master. Mom wanted me to go to university, but university in the mid-1960s required Grade 13. For me that meant repeating Grade 12. And Nora was now in Grade 13. I just had to convince Mom.

Now, facing her dumbed-down daughter, Mom regroups. I can see the thoughts jumping through her head as she frowns.

"Hmm," she says, pursing her lips. She lets out a sigh. "Well, we have some money saved from the baby bonus. All right, but you have to phone the school guidance and tell them you're not coming back."

I'm too shy to do this, but force myself to sit at the black rotary phone in the dark corner of the dining room and dial.

So I go to Shaw Business College for one year and quit one subject short of finishing. Mom has now succumbed to one of the family curses—arthritis. It is my turn to bring bread and cake into the house. Besides, I have redeemed my educational standing. Typing, Pitman Shorthand, normal math including bookkeeping, business English, spelling, and power reading are all subjects I enjoy. They contain enough teeth to challenge me and my marks shoot up from the 50s in Grade 12 to the 90s. I also start to lose some of the "baby fat," so dominant around my middle the previous couple of years. I experiment with clothes and makeup, although with the weight loss, the skirts develop puckered waistlines.

During my last day at Shaw, the school's branch manager calls me into her office for my exit interview. She is in her mid-forties, with short dark hair, and despite glasses, she looks like an aging slut. She wears short tight skirts, has a big bust and a voice that would leave Kim Novak standing silent at an audition.

"Are you sure you want to leave when you are almost finished?" she asks.

"Yes. My mother isn't well," I say. "So I have to get out and work."

"Oh, I'm sorry," she says. "Okay, then. As you know, we set you up with a few job interviews for openings that have come in to the school. I have one here for the Ontario government with the Department of Mines. It's in their map service office and they need a secretary. It's an all-male office, so you'll be Queen Bee."

I nod as she hands me a piece of paper with the information.

"You will phone a Jeffrey Stone at this number for an interview. He is the manager of that section. It's in the Whitney Block at Queen's Park."

"Thank you."

"And Sharon, I wouldn't wear that beige lipstick. Wear something in a light red or dark pink."

I am livid. I have regular coloured lipstick, but I like the beige. But I don't say anything to this would-be aging sexpot. Thanking her again, I stand up to my five foot one and with all the brashness of my nearly 19 years, stride out of her office.

The job is mine, and during the year working there, I meet the man I will later marry. But not before deciding to make up for lost time in the fun and dating department. The hunting is good for a young girl in an all-male office, an office more Peyton or Melrose Place than staid Ontario government.

Our office was called the League of Nations because we had a variety of nationalities—Japanese, Italian, Irish, Scottish, English, Polish and a few of us Canadians. Three male clerks—one Italian, one Irish, and one Scottish, along with a fourth and fifth during the summer—another Italian, and my British boyfriend-to-be shared the tiny outer office with me and a table where the visiting geologists could spread out the maps and look at them. The clerks' job was to get the maps for the geologists while I pounded out letters and file cards on an old manual typewriter. Where was the electric typewriter like the one I practiced on at Shaw? So, the clerks and I had to either retreat from each other or bond. We bonded to the point where during a lull in work we would discuss serious issues such as dating.

Antonio, the summer Italian guy, is presenting his discourse on what he wants in a woman. He leans over his desk like it is a pulpit and stares at each of us one-by-one.

"She must be pretty, blond. She must..."

I try to tune him out but my ears are ringing. Who is this ego-god no older than my 19 years who dares to preach? Does he expect us to kneel to his views? Not me. I shove my chair back, banging it against the wall, jump up and stomp over to where he sits at the desk in the corner—barely three feet away—and glare up at him.

"You don't want a girlfriend. You want a paragon." With another glare, I swing around, stomp out of the office and down the hall to the Ladies Room.

The other Italian guy, Joe, is like a brother, a nice brother who prances into the room, nose straight out in the air beyond here, mouth compressed and eyes staring directly ahead. He wears a long-sleeved white shirt—sometimes with narrow black stripes, pressed black pants, polished black shoes, and carries a slick black briefcase which he places under his desk. At lunch, he puts the briefcase on his desk, opens it, and removes his lunch—chocolate sandwiches on white bread.

These two men did not join the parade of men I dated during that year. Counting the fellow I became engaged to, I dated four men (at different times) from this place of work—but only two were in my actual office. The other two were in another government department connected to the Department of Mines. But still too close for common sense comfort. It never entered my head that maybe some truth existed in what the principal at Holy Cross said about me at the end of Grade 8. "Sharon has no common sense." Sharon also had no big sister to steer her around the dating circuit. A big sister could have warned me about the perils of dating someone from the same office. Perhaps she would have made an exception with my soon-to-be fiancé because he worked there only during the summer; after the summer we met, I was long gone from the Department of Mines.

Or would my mythical big sister have stepped in and yelled, "Hey, Sharon, 13 years older?" when I went out with Grant. Would she have pointed out the warning signs shooting invisibly from Grant—acting boss when Mr. Stone was away, never married and still living at home? Or would she have held her breath until it was over and it *was* over after three months.

However, dating Grant came back to haunt me that summer after I began dating the man I would marry.

The clerks and I are sitting around in the office when Christine, the predecessor in my job, strolls in to gossip. The conversation gets around to the usual topic. Christine starts a rant about *l'affaire de Grant et Sharon*, although it never went beyond dating and the occasional kiss.

"It was so funny," she is saying.

I cover my face with my hands as if that would hide it all from my fiancé-to-be, sitting on the other side of my desk. I never told him about Grant.

"You nosy gossip," Grant is telling her.

The rest is a blur. But the next scene is with Grant and me alone in the office.

"Don't let her bother you," he says. "I've seen her sitting in a car necking with the guy she dates."

It never occurs to me how Grant would know this. Later I will wonder. Was he the man in the car? Was he spying on Christine? Or more probably, did Christine blab and brag?

I am still blundering around in dating land. I can't talk to Mom about this. She really won't know what to say. She's a farm girl, after all. Too bad I didn't know then that Mom had only snagged Dapper Albert, a ladies' man when he was 40 and she was 32.

***

My social life isn't just dating. Technically, I still fit in the age group of the 15-20 Club, but I am out of school and working 9 to 5. It seems like a natural progression when on a Sunday after one of the few Masses I attend at Holy Cross, Father T. the assistant pastor approaches me about joining the Working Girls Club he runs. Ruth receives the same invitation.

We never meet at the church but at members' houses. We are a small bunch of women of various shapes, sizes, jobs, ages and outlooks. The focus is discussion on a topic relevant to our lives as young women in the world, with an unhealthy dollop of church teaching.

One evening the meeting is in the living room at my place. Mother is downstairs watching TV in the rec room. Ruth and I sit on the split chesterfield; two other women are in chairs pulled in from the dining room. Father T. sits in the chair under the window. Beatrice slouches in the rose-coloured easy chair by the World Book Encyclopedias. She ignores the books; instead she stares at Father T. as he goes on about the Vatican's latest pronouncement on birth control. Beatrice lurches her 5 foot dumpy body up straight in the chair, digs her hands into the armrests and puts on a calculated smile. She pushes back a strand of her short blond hair and glares through her rectangular glasses. Then she opens her mouth.

"No Pope is coming into my bedroom and telling me what to do and not do," she says.

Silence hits the room. She is too outspoken and maybe that's why she frightens me. She seems sophisticated, too sure of herself, and probably pegs me as green and immature.

Father T. decides we need a break from our monthly discussions. He arranges a night out on the town. We carpool,—Ruth and I with him,—I refuse to ride with Beatrice—to a medieval restaurant in downtown Toronto. Throughout the evening of feigned debauchery—eating with our fingers, putting up with a few insults from the wenches who serve us, and a handsome balladeer, guitar in hand, weaving his way from table to table, the situation of "to drink or not to drink" arises.

Ruth and I are the only underage "Working Girls" present. My only claim to drinking alcohol goes back four years when Mom, Daddy and I visited their friends, the Pratts—a couple around their age, with a son, Brett, five years older than me. Brett took our drink orders and brought my grape juice all right, except it was the fermented kind. I was furious.

The legal drinking age is 21 and I aim to keep to it. I have to be seen as the good girl or I will go to hell, both on earth with a damaged reputation and afterwards in ever-ever land. I also want to appear grown-up, so at this medieval dinner I order a Shirley Temple. Ruth does the same. Our drinks arrive in goblets and I ride high on the sophistication horse.

"Shirley Temples, eh?" Beatrice sneers at the pink liquid.

I stare down at the table.

These tables take a bizarre turn, however, when we leave for home. I'm not sure about Beatrice, but our driver, Father T. is laughing and patting a few of us on the shoulders. As we follow his weaving figure out the door into the parking lot, my heart sinks into my stomach. I don't want to get into his car but I don't have the nerve to say "au revoir" and take a streetcar and bus home. Ruth seems to have the same idea, so we climb into the back seat and shut the doors.

Father T. inserts the ignition key, turns it, and the car jolts forward.

"Hee. Hee. Whoopee." He races the car forward, hair-spins around some parked cars, then lurches into one of the parking lot aisles. "Whee. This is fun. Hee. Hee."

He reverses the car and it shoots backwards. Ruth and I clutch the sides of the back seats as if that will keep us anchored. Every jerk of the car bumps us up, then down, and our heads careen forward, sideways, and back.

"Dear God," I pray. "Please don't let us have an accident."

Father zigzags the car out onto Dundas Street and hits the accelerator.

"Please God, don't have us get arrested," I whisper.

We make it back to my place. Mumbling a "thank you" to Father and "I'll call you tomorrow" to Ruth, I run into the house.

Ruth makes it home safely. So does Father. Years later I will learn that he was an alcoholic, which had something to do with his death.

Not all my non-date outings were with runaway priests. When our birthdays came around in November and December, Mom and I took each other out to dinner, often at the Superior Restaurant in downtown Toronto or at a restaurant that once existed a few doors east of the Bloor-Yonge subway entrance on the north side of Bloor Street. At the latter, I had my first taste of many-course meals with sides of cheese in between, and apple pie and ice cream with coffee or tea to finish it off. We also went to the buffet upstairs in The Arcadian Room at Simpsons Department Store where I learned the art of all-you-can-eat buffet dining. My boyfriend, his best friend from university, and I sometimes ate at the latter. I think that's the first time I experienced a bloated abdomen.

When this boyfriend, the one I am going to marry, returns to McGill the fall after we met, I quit my job with the Ontario Government and take a month off between jobs. I alternate between moping and crying around the apartment Mom and I share, and travelling to Montreal. When I decide to start job-hunting I go to the Drake Agency, then a small one-office business in an old downtown Toronto building.

."Why did you take a month off?" the interviewing agent asks. "It doesn't look good on the resume."

"I…er… I…needed a vacation."

Maybe that's why she saddles me with the secretarial job in an insurance agency's office. A one-person agency with me making it two, although I may as well be the one person, because this agent is out 95 per cent of the time and when in, he says little.

Mr. Marks is in his late 50s, tall, a gentleman, but not a teacher, not a motivator to get his secretary to type letters, insurance contracts and riders, and actually care about doing so.

"Here's some contracts to type up," he says. He hands me some blank forms and his scribbled notes on a legal-sized pad. "There's a rider on this one for furs and jewellery." He points with his lighted cigarette to his notes and the blank rider. "And I have a couple of letters to dictate to go with them."

He goes over to his desk and sits down. I haul out my shorthand book but this is not a real Pittman workout.

"Dear Mrs. Cunningham," he dictates in his soft wavering voice. "Further to our discussion of yesterday's date, please find enclosed the insurance policy for your property." He pauses and inhales on his cigarette.

It gives me time to get ahead of him—pencil poised above my steno pad. I sneak a glance at him. He is smiling as he continues to dictate the letter.

He doesn't smile for long. His wife has cancer, he mentions one day, but goes into few details except to say she is in the hospital. I know this is not good and can't seem to say anything sympathetic, but *should* be able to. Daddy was about the same age as my boss when he was first diagnosed and he smoked, too. Although never having met my boss's wife, I don't know her age, don't know if she even smokes. I remain silent and just look at him, hoping my face wears sympathy.

A few weeks later he comes in late. His wrinkles looked more pinched than usual, and his face also wears a pallor—as if he has seen the other side of life and it has left him behind, with a tenuous hold on the living side.

"Mary died," he says. His mouth wavers into an upside-down smile and I cannot resist sneaking a peek at his eyes. Yes, there are tears.

"I am sorry for your loss," I mumble and stare at my hands.

He mentions something about arranging for the funeral and that he will be out of the office for the next three days.

"You're in charge. If anyone calls, just take messages. I'll get back to them later." His voice is now a shaky eulogy as if he is practicing for her funeral.

I don't ask him where and when the funeral is. I won't be going. But I check it out in the OB's in the daily newspaper.

Shortly after, I go away for the long Easter weekend to join Mom and Great Aunt Hilda who are visiting Aunt Minnie in Detroit. In 1969 much had changed since my last visit. Not only had Uncle Terry died in July 1967, but the same month Detroit suffered through five days of perhaps its worse riots. During the 1960s, racial issues reached the boiling point throughout the USA. Early on Sunday morning, July 23, 1967, Detroit police engaged in one of their usual blind pig raids—hitting illegal drinking spots in east-end Detroit. Instead of hauling in a token number of found-ins, this time the police busted all 85 of them at 12th and Clairmont. The wait for more paddy wagons in the humid pre-dawn raised tempers and started shouts of "police brutality." The few hundred curious people soon escalated into thousands. The riot was on. Over the next days, it spread past 12th to

Linwood and skirted close to Woodward. The rioters burned and looted buildings, and hoarded guns. The federal government called in the National Guard. If Mom and I had visited her friend in Windsor and looked across the Detroit River, we would have smelled the smoke and seen the firefighters' ladders angled up into the flames. The Boblo Island boat that Mom and I once cruised on, stayed docked, with 30 crew members only, for two nights at Windsor.[19] The statistical tally rang in at 2,509 buildings looted and burned, 7,231 arrested, 467 injured, and 43 dead.[20] The psychological tally cannot be measured, although if you talked to Aunt Minnie and Laurie afterwards, fear became a way of life. Their neighbourhood had deteriorated and the east-end's racial mess and poverty had spilled over into the west. Over the following years, it affected my aunt and cousins. One evening, Minnie and Laurie had their purses snatched as they opened their front door. The house was broken into once. Laurie was mugged four times, once at gunpoint in the field next to their place.

So, on my post-Uncle Terry visit two years after his death, I pick up on this fear. At 20, I am supposed to be an adult, but feel more like a 10-year-old journeying through a foreign country. The train now stops at Windsor, but Windsor station sits in Walkerville out in the burbs and I haven't a clue where that is. From Walkerville, I get on a bus to cross the border. The bus will stop at two downtown hotels but Mom has made arrangements for Cousin Gordon to pick me up at Detroit's train station. Downtown Detroit hotels aren't safe, she says, but as the bus turns into the train station I don't like the bleak look outside. I also don't like that the bus arrives early. My whole body drags down the bus steps and this has nothing to do with

---

[19] From stories in *The Windsor Star*, July 25, 1967.

[20] Edwards, Chris, and Weeks, Elaine, "Black Day In July," *Walkerville Times*. Online. [Accessed November 25, 2019] http://www.walkervilletimes.com/26/black-day-july.html. Compiled from stories in *The Detroit News: Rearview Mirror* www.detnews.com/history/index.html.

carting a big purse and heavy suitcase. I am also carrying a big case of dread. Inside the train station, a few people, blacks and whites, go about their business and I hope their business has nothing to do with me. I hang onto my purse and suitcase as if they are sewn to my hands and take a few quick cautious looks around.

Where is Cousin Gordon?

I ease myself down on a bench as far away as possible from its only other occupant and keep hands on baggage and purse. Periodically, I scan the room and its unfamiliar occupants, glance at the wall clock, and clutch my purse tighter.

Then I see Gordon and sigh with relief.

Three days later I return alone to Toronto. Mom and Great Aunt Hilda stay a little longer. Monday morning I am back in the insurance agency office. However, soon I will resign. The work is sparse, boring, and unchallenging. There is no one around to connect with. Certainly not my boss. Not with the cancer and his smoking cigarette hovering in the air between us. It is only three and a half years since Daddy died and I don't need reminders.

22: Seeing Through Blue-coloured Glasses

You don't have to be crazy to work here but it sure helps.
—**Old Anonymous Saying**

My father-in-law-to-be comes up with the solution. He works as a clerk at Toronto Police headquarters. At his suggestion, I apply for a clerical position at the Toronto Police Force and get hired as a temporary clerk in the Morality Bureau.

I like my job, the quirky cops and civilians. Female police officers are new to the force and any I see at headquarters are cadets. This means that sometimes we civilians are allowed to help with real police work.

Back in 1969, abortions were still illegal. Two morality detectives set me up to help them catch an abortionist. They are outside the building housing the doctor's office when one of them calls me at the Morality Bureau. He tells me to pretend I need an abortion. However, he doesn't want me to go to the doctor's office, but to phone there and find out if Dr. Abortionist is in. If he is, they will charge inside and arrest him. So, he gives me the doctor's phone number, makes sure I am clear on what to do, then hangs up. I grab at the chance to do some undercover work, and dial.

My phone spiel goes over well, but Dr. Abortionist is not in. The two detectives don't arrest him on my watch, but do so a few weeks later at night when I am at home, sleeping.

One of the ladies I hang around with at lunchtime, Andrea, also is "hired" by the morality detectives to trap a fake fortune-teller. They choose her because she speaks Italian. She pretends to be the fortune-teller's client. Then the detectives arrest the fraudster.

Two other Morality detectives ride on the same subway to work as I do, and often we run into each other. These two like to clown around, and their antics make me laugh. We usually exit the subway at Sherbourne and walk to the old police headquarters at 590 Jarvis Street. The subways are crowded, and like today, inconsiderate people block the doorways, even when there is some room inside.

Detective G. and Detective J. decide to make an example of a door-blocker. When the subway arrives at Sherbourne Station and the doors slide open, the detective duo each grab one of the man's arms and drag him outside the car onto the platform. They hold him there until the train doors close. The hapless man is standing there, looking perplexed as the train roars out of the station. I wait nearby on the platform and laugh.

But Detectives G's and J's antics don't escape me. If we run into each other on the subway, the three of us walk together from Sherbourne to 590 Jarvis Street. We turn down Jarvis Street and when we arrive at the Mount Pleasant crossing, they say, "You're not moving fast enough." They each grab an arm and half drag and half lift me across the street. Yes, I laugh. But I feel safe being guided by two detective across a busy street.

Morality also includes cannabis (possession was illegal at the time) and other drug offences. For some reason there is a marijuana plant sitting in a big planter in the office. Perhaps to help for identification? One day, I am up at the file cabinet wall, filing liquor license permits. My back is to the office. Suddenly, a pungent smell permeates the air. When I swing around I see smoke coming from the pot plant. One of the detectives is burning it.

It isn't all fun and games, but because I am temporary civilian staff, my sojourn in Morality has to end sometime.

The Staff Sergeant writes a glowing recommendation for me to go permanent with the police force. However, there are no vacant clerical positions in Morality—the two clerks I temped for, one right after the other, are back, so I get transferred as secretary to the data processing section. This permanent status means a medical is required, and that terrifies me. Not only do I not want to pee in a bottle or a pitcher as Mom did for her urine test, there is also worry over what the doctor might find. I know it has to do with Mom now in the hospital for her own medical prodding for arthritis.

I have slid into a routine—go to work, visit Mom, then return home to an empty apartment. My spirit seizes up and my body fights to protect it. Daily, I consume grilled cheese sandwiches, baked beans, an apple, and coffee, perhaps figuring if I don't eat much it is a sacrifice, so Mom will get better. The worry and diet cause my weight to nosedive, something that works against me at work. By now, I have a continuous headache and fail the department's glorified eye test. It is not my eyes the department's doctor takes a hit at; it is my weight of 90 pounds, as if *that* will stop me from doing a good job. I haven't missed a day as a temp. He says he'll hold passing my medical until I gain 10 pounds.

My family doctor tells me the pain in my head is because I need glasses and to get my eyes tested.

"I don't want to get my eyes tested," I tell Mom, the next evening when visiting her at St. Michael's. "I don't want eye drops because they blind you."

When my fiancé had his eyes tested with drops, he kept seeing pink elephants, and I had to guide him back to work. Who's going to hang on to me? He's back at McGill University in Montreal, and Mom lies in a hospital bed.

The three ladies in Mom's ward come up with a solution.

"Go across the street from here and get your eyes tested there. They don't use drops on young girls."

So, after visiting Mom, I cross Queen Street. I don't stride in sturdy like steel, but shake like a drug addict arriving for a fix.

"Do you use eye drops?" I ask.

"No," says the receptionist and smiles at me.

I frown, still wary that the eye doctor will start squirting liquid into my eyes. He doesn't, and my next stop is the Optician Section to get fitted for glasses. After a one-hour wait, I put them on. This is the closest I will ever get to standing tall, as the floor appears miles below me. Outside it starts to snow and it feels like walking on stilts so I take extra care to avoid slipping in the flakes as they touch the sidewalk.

The next evening I waltz into Mom's ward to show off my glasses. My headache has disappeared and the correct perception of height has returned. My weight starts increasing, but that's because Mom is coming home.

Finally my weight rises sufficiently for the doctor to rubber stamp my medical. Officially, I am permanent civilian staff. Soon Data Processing becomes part of a larger section called Departmental Support Services—a blend of cops and civilians. Because I am now engaged, there is no worry about mixing dating and working. I am after friends to hang around with, or so I think, but it will turn into a see-saw in more ways than one.

At first the other female clerk, Lynn, senior to me in classification, years on the job and eight years older than me, is cordial. Unlike the three older women in Morality, with their quirks and faults, two of whom had looked out for me like I was their favourite niece, Lynn has a hidden side. It doesn't surface until after the incident with Cindy the clerk who starts working in the section shortly after me.

After playing new kid on the block, it is my turn to give back, so at Lynn's suggestion I take Cindy under my wing. We go to breaks and lunch together in the police cafeteria. . . .

I am getting a mouth on me sometimes but words only slip out occasionally. Cindy and I enter the cafeteria at break. She gets her coffee and sits down at a table. I dawdle, adding milk and sugar to my coffee. I am carrying a sweater in my left hand and have my purse slung over my right shoulder. Being right-handed, I grab my coffee with my right hand and stride over to the table to join Cindy. When leaning over, before I can even think about setting my coffee cup down, my purse strap slides down my arm, purse collides with hand, sending the coffee spurting out. The cup stays put but my mouth doesn't.

"Shit," I say loudly.

Cindy stares down at the table and doesn't say much, and I'm too embarrassed to apologize. I get a couple of paper towels and wipe up the mess. This time I stay quiet and tell myself it wasn't my fault; my purse skidded.

From then on Cindy pretends she doesn't know me and she starts hanging out with Lynn on coffee breaks and lunch. I am sure she has had a heart-to-heart with Lynn, expanding on the coffee-swearing incident. Lynn starts playing double personality with me—nice on the surface when others are up close, but mean when it comes to handing out work, and chastising me for not being perfect.

One day she gets in her nasty-nice stride, chewing me out. If others weren't nearby, she would probably have spit me out. She doesn't have to bother. I am already out the door and down the elevator to the main floor and into the Employment Office, which is also under the Departmental Support Services section.

I am practically in tears as I beg one of the sergeant's for work. He seems to have a soft spot for me so I complain to him about Lynn. I have no clue that this is all office politics but get him on my side.

Cindy transfers to another department and Myra transfers in. She has as much service time as Lynn, but she is my age and treats everyone the same—in a friendly respectful manner. She and I get along, but don't hang around. She is friends with Lynn from way back, so she takes breaks with her and Cindy.

I spend breaks with Andrea, discovering she is another only child who is ostracized somewhat. I'm not sure if it is her nationality—Italian—or her job; she doesn't type so she operates the photocopier. But when it comes right down to it, I think it's because she's not pretty. She has a curvaceous figure, no extra fat, but people can't seem to get past a face with pimples and a big nose. Andrea and I get along fine.

But most days we have different lunch periods. I have the earlier lunch. I start hanging around with the two clerks in the stores unit where my father-in-law-to-be works—another Lynn and a Clem—as well as Rich, the clerk in the Auto Squad, and Dina, one of the many clerks in Records. We are all either just married or getting married—it seems to be contagious, but it's really what most young people did in the early 1970s. When we thought we had found Mr. or Ms. Right, we didn't move in together, we got married, whether we knew what we were doing or not.

When Myra gets engaged and her wedding nears, I make sure I'm in charge of arranging her wedding present from the office. I want to do this because she treats me decently but also think I need to be in charge of something office-related. Because Lynn is Myra's friend and the senior clerk in our section, the wedding gift technically should be her responsibility. But it is my job now, so I take special care looking at gifts and figuring out what style would suit Myra.

My turn is coming up. My fiancé and I plan a May 1972 wedding.

But just when you think everything is looking up, you forget to stare down at reality.

Mom is now spiraling closer to Dad's age when he died, spiraling down, hitting obstacles, and picking up much pain along the way. It has been going on even before we moved to the apartment.

Part Six: Endings And Beginnings

Sharon in her late teens, with Mom

On the Steps of Holy Cross Church

23: Suddenly

Time is a cruel thief to rob us of our former selves. We lose as much to life as we do to death.
—**Elizabeth Forsythe Hailey,** *A Woman of Independent Means*

"Look at the bereaved." The priest waves his hand. "Would Julia's daughter like to come up and show her grief?"

I want to dig my nails into his heart. Instead I grip the back of the pew in front and shake my head. Excuse me, Father, you convert to Catholicism, this is my mother's funeral. Show some respect. I take a quick look at Aunt Minnie, my godmother, and Cousin Gordon behind me. Holy funeral Mass, and Father, did they do this in your former religion?

I hope Mom's spirit is hovering, ready to clout him. This priest was not my first pick to officiate. His weird funeral protocol only confirms my decision to have the pastor marry my fiancé and me. This priest standing at the front of the church refused to marry a couple of my friends because their fiancés were not Catholic. I wonder if before conducting Mom's funeral he did a check of her religious background.

He wouldn't have found anything to complain about—baptized a Catholic, November 10, 1907, Immaculate Conception Church, Formosa, Ontario, married a Catholic in St. Anthony's Catholic Church, Toronto, November 25, 1939, daughter baptized a Catholic, December 12, 1948 in Holy Cross Church, where today, August 7, 1971, he is performing his abomination. He can't know about my blasphemous confession a couple of years before. Priests are supposed to honour the seal of the confession. That particular confession occurred between his predecessor, Father T. and me. My so-called confession, where I did more questioning than confessing, morphed into a contest of wills. We argued about the nature of sin.

"Don't you have to have the intent to do something for it to be a mortal sin?" I asked.

Father T. snarled. "So, if you kill someone without the intent to do so, it isn't a sin?"

I'm not sure what the intent of this priest conducting Mom's funeral is. Perhaps he is trying to embarrass me and demean my mother. Why?

***

I guess I gave Mom a hard time with religion during the last few years of her life. She still went to church every Sunday. When we moved in 1968 to the apartment, our windows faced Holy Cross Church, a short block away. But my partial dumping of religion started while we still lived at 139. Sunday mornings we'd wrangle over whether I would or wouldn't go to church.

My saving grace was that I liked folk music and old buildings. With Pope John XXIII reigning over the Catholic Church during the hippie movement, acoustic guitars and folksy hymns started showing up at Catholic Masses throughout Toronto. Some of the folk singers at Holy Cross were former classmates, but that didn't always lure me in. Sometimes the battle royal with Mom ended with us going our separate ways—her to Holy Cross and me on public transit to the folk Mass at St. Paul's Basilica on Power Street in downtown Toronto.

Our religious bickering gave Mom little comfort after Daddy died. Mom, who could manage finances and budgets like a VP of Finance and garden like a master, had lost her soul mate. Although, during the last four years of Dad's life, we had expected him to die, when it happened, Mom didn't do widowhood very well.

She had already reconnected with her former colleagues, currently executives at the insurance company she worked at before my birth. Now she toiled there as a typist. But her professional and personal life began twisting into limbo. One of the Strauss family curses began seeping through her bones. Like her mother, she developed rheumatoid arthritis, but unlike her mother, she refused to spend her days in bed. Instead, she dragged herself into the office.

Rheumatoid arthritis battered her feet first with swelling, aching and distortion. When the arthritis spread to her hands, her boss switched her from typing to proofreading. And another disease with a hard-to-remember and an even harder-to-spell name also invaded her body. Scleroderma.

Scleroderma is "an autoimmune disease affecting the blood vessels and connective tissue, occurring most often in middle-aged women. Skin changes in the face and fingers and rheumatoid-arthritis-like symptoms progress to areas where the skin becomes fixed to underlying tissue. In severe cases the skin of the face may become so taut as to interfere with chewing and swallowing. Treatment includes corticosteroids and analgesics."[21]

Mom sure fit the scleroderma bill. Her cheeks puffed up like the proverbial chipmunk, except they felt hard to the touch. She managed to eat and swallow, but her voice turned into a reedy fragment of its former crisp self. She also missed days and weeks of work.

She is on a mini-leave of absence when I arrive home from work where I find two strange men with her in the living room. They are both sitting on the chesterfield, one on either side of its designed split. Mom is in the pink chair by the bookcase as if the World Books standing guard behind can lift her up beyond the swollen foot propped on a footstool. The conversation stops and the two men stare at me with blank smiles on their faces.

"This is Peter McLaren and this is John Vardis from Surety Insurance." Mom points to each. "This is my daughter, Sharon."

"Hello." I plop down in the chair under the window.

The men say, "Hello," nod; then McLaren continues the conversation.

"Julia," he says. "I know you are a valuable employee but we need to know if you are coming back to work."

---

[21] Rothenberg, Mikel A., MD, and Charles F. Chapman. *Dictionary of Medical Terms*, Third Edition, Hauppauge, NY, Barron's Educational Series, Inc., 1994.

"I don't like to say it, but I have to," Vardis says. "It might be better if you retired now." He addresses the mantle.

"Let's not be hasty, John," McLaren says, and then looks Mom right in the eye. "Julia, do you think you will be able to come back?"

"I don't know." Mom's voice is wispy and little girlish.

I grip the arms of the chair and don't even have the courage to wish one of the men would shuffle around in the chesterfield so it would move at the split. That might jolt them.

I can't stop staring at my mother's feet. The near normal one wears a slipper, but the other one is raw, swollen, and bare except for the gauze wrapped around the ankle and heel. Mom splays her deformity on the footstool as if to will these hard-nosed executives to show some compassion and stop messing around with her future.

The conversation stops and I jerk my eyes away from the feet. The men stand up. The chesterfield stays intact. McLaren crosses the room and pats Mom on the shoulder. "Well, you think about it, Julia, and let us know," he says.

They leave and I look over at Mom. She cowers in the chair as if she's just received the death penalty. I still can't grasp the seriousness of it. It doesn't occur to me then that I could later travel down a similar road as Mom.

Mom soon hands in her resignation. At least I'm working, I rationalize.

During this time, Mom also makes the difficult decision to sell the house and move into a two-bedroom apartment. Of course I am going with her and also become her reluctant help to get us out of the house.

I am lying on that living-room chesterfield. My ears are tuned to the top 40 bleating from the radio and the rest of my face and mind are buried in an Agatha Christie mystery.

"Sharon, help me clear out this stuff downstairs. What are we going to do with it all?" Mom shouts up from the basement.

"In a minute," I reply, telling myself I will just read to the end of this chapter.

"Sharon."

"Be there in a minute."

"Sharon."

"All right."

I shove a bookmark in the Agatha Christie, place it on the end table and stomp down the basement stairs, around the sharp curve midway. At least I won't have to look at the orange stucco stairwell walls much longer. What was Daddy thinking when he painted them?

I am ashamed of my thoughts, and as if to make amends, dig into the latest box of stored possessions. This carton, tall, narrow, and heavy, contains my school exercise books, drawings, high school yearbooks, and newspapers.

"Do you want all of this?" Mom asks. "You decide."

But I don't care what happens to all this excess stuff. I just want to get out of this stifling house where there is little room to manoeuvre through the furniture and dust bunnies. Its bricks, tiles, and mortar couldn't keep Daddy safe. It never occurs to me that 139 might also be mourning a loss.

But it has gained in value since my parents, its first owners, bought it and paid "$22 a month with the privilege of paying an additional $175 annually," according to the faded print in the letter from the insurance company holding the first mortgage. That letter is dated July 5, 1943.

From the lawyer's letter to Mom about the sale of 139 in 1968:

You agreed to sell this property for $24,500.00 and a deposit of $1,000.00 was paid to the real estate agent, when the offer to purchase was submitted. The purchaser agreed to pay the balance of the purchase price on closing subject to adjustments.

I transport some of our belongings, with the help of my fiancé. We load my record player and records into Mom's bundle buggy and wheel it the six blocks to the apartment building Mom and I will soon call home. On Moving Day, men from Tippet-Richardson, the big moving company, show up, pack clothes and dishes and transport everything to the two-bedroom apartment. Only the sugar bowl lid gets broken, and they reimburse Mom for its damage.

From the lawyer's letter to Mom about the sale of 139:

Your sale of the above property was completed on June 21ˢᵗ 1968 with adjustments being made to June 28ᵗʰ 1968 the agreed closing date.

While continuing my work life, I can't escape Mom's macabre transformation. Her fingers bend more and she whines a lot. Her worry jumps over to me. When her doctor admits her to the hospital for tests, I figure we have reached the end of the road. My vision and work medical issues running concurrently do not make it any easier. However, she is nearly 62 years to my nearly 21 years, so age has a factor in the development and outcome of her diseases. If only a new pair of glasses could make her better, like they did for me.

I don't know then that eye tests and headaches will also factor into Mom's medical conditions.

So I'm making yet another visit to the hallowed and disinfected halls of St. Michael's Hospital, and enter Mom's ward. She looks lost and diminished in the bed. Taking a deep breath, I grab a chair and sit down.

"Hi Mom. How are you?" I ask.

"The doctors had trouble finding anywhere on my fingers or arm to prick for blood tests because my skin is so tough from the arthritis and the scleroderma." Mom's voice sounds small and she seems to disappear even further into the stark hospital bed. "So, they pricked my ear."

The medical tests reaffirm she has arthritis and scleroderma. After being released from the hospital, she starts pumping up on more and stronger cortisone pills and now has appointments to keep with our family doctor, a podiatrist for her feet, and occasionally one of the few rheumatologists practising in the late 1960s.

***

"What do you want for dinner tonight?" Mom asks. She's been home from the hospital for a few months. "Steak okay?"

"Sure."

The Enemies Within Us

"Okay. I'll take the steak out of the freezer."

Instead she takes out the bacon and I have the nerve to scold her about it. But I'm not all bad. I'm giving her part of my salary to pay for the food, and with her help, learning to plan menus and do a grocery list, based on the specials at the different grocery stores. I wheel the bundle buggy up the street to the IGA. Sometimes if it is early enough I don't need the buggy—they will deliver. Or I go further up the street to the Loblaws.

***

One bleak evening in April 1971 Mom is alone at the apartment because I am out cruising the cafes with a girlfriend. Mom spends her evenings slouched in an armchair, which she pulls up close to the TV so she can watch reruns of *Marcus Welby, MD* in black and white. When I return, she is asleep in bed, but the next morning she tells me what happened.

"I fell off my vanity bench and banged my head on the floor," she says. "I'm okay."

Although Mom likes and approves of my fiancé, she has an ongoing rant with herself and me about where she will live after I move out. In summer, she makes several trips to visit her sister, my godmother, on the farm near Lucknow. She travels by bus with her 80-something Aunt Hilda, who has more spunk and life in her than Mom. I go along for one of the rides early in that summer of 1971. I don't remember much of this trip, but Mom makes sure to tell me about another of her trips that summer.

"I fell going down the steps outside the house," she says. Her sister's house has only two steps. "I'm okay now, just a couple of bruises on my leg." I still don't connect the dots, even when she adds, "Sharon, I don't know whether I should live with my sister on the farm for the summer and just come back here for the winter."

For a change, she's sitting in the chesterfield and she looks sunk and lost. She is holding out a line for help but the line is outside my vision. Perhaps remembering Daddy's long and gradual decline has frozen any care and caregiving genes. Now 22, engaged, with a good job, don't I deserve my "happily ever after?" So I just nod and look at her.

Coward.

"Maybe I should move into a one-bedroom here but I just renewed the lease on this apartment, so it's good until the end of next June." She seems to be staring straight through my eyes as if she can harvest some strength from my mind. Mom, I'm still a scaredy-cat. You and Daddy protected me too well.

Coward.

I seem to forget about our leaning on each other during Daddy's journey through cancer. Despite pulling away from Daddy emotionally, thanks to an inner voice, I steered Mom to his bedside when he was dying.

But not with Mom. Am I again pulling away? The signs are all there. I just don't see them. Just don't get it. Not even when her falls come back to haunt her and she complains about headaches.

"It's just my eyes," she says. "I probably need new glasses." Her explanation seems to make sense so I accept it without question.

Big mistake.

She books an appointment with her ophthalmologist for September, the earliest date available.

The last Saturday morning in July, I get up at my regular late time of 9.30. I hear nothing and don't smell the coffee Mom usually makes when she rises at 7 a.m. I wonder what's going on and step out to the living room and dining room. She is not there. She isn't in the bathroom either, but when I push open her bedroom door she is still lying in bed.

"Mom, why aren't you up? Come on, get up." I charge over to the bed. She is lying on her back; her eyes are closed, and she appears to be still asleep, so I shake her. "Mom, stop playing tricks and get up. This isn't funny." She doesn't move, but she's still breathing.

Oh, no. What do I do? Why won't she open her eyes? What *is* going on?

I dash out to the living room and yank the phone off the cradle. My heart does double-time and I want my mind to go to numb. Each turn of the dial stretches each number into a long road to uncertainty.

I manage to get the doctor's office. His answering service picks up. They'll leave him a message. They don't think it's urgent, but I'm at my wits end. I don't know why she won't wake up, but cannot deal with the situation alone. So, I call my fiancé and he rushes over.

Wishful thinking. He has just moved out of his parents' apartment into a studio apartment. His phone isn't installed yet and his parents don't have a phone. So, I call his landlady and leave a convoluted message. My fiancé arrives just before the doctor—in the early afternoon, hours after I found Mom.

"Looks like a stroke," the doctor says when he examines her. "I'll call an ambulance and she'll have to go to St. Mike's."

My mind and heart fly all over the place. When the ambulance arrives, the attendants wheel Mom out on a gurney. They take the nearest elevator, and the doctor, my fiancé, and I walk down the hall to the other one. Downstairs, the doctor says he'll meet us at the hospital. Outside, the sun shines; the cars whiz by on a typical Cosburn Avenue day, except for the ambulance intruding in front of the apartment building. When the attendants wheel Mom inside, I feel the normalness in my life veering off into unknown territory. If I look down, the sidewalk will move from under my feet sending me tumbling down, down, down.

My fiancé steers me towards the ambulance to ride with Mom, but my mind disappears and doesn't surface until we race into the hospital ER. I see the nurse on duty, June, my nurse-cousin Felicity's best friend. I have a momentary feeling of hope as if familiarity breeds cures. But St. Michael must have only half a wing turned towards us, because when the doctor arrives, they aren't going to let him in. They say he's not accredited at the hospital and for the first and only time I see him kick up a fuss. June sees us, intervenes and sorts it out. Later, while my fiancé, his mom (who has joined us) and I sit in blue vinyl chairs and stare at lemon yellow walls, June enters carrying Mom's belongings.

A paper bag with a soiled nightgown. Is that all she has to show for 63 years?

"What do I do if she's a vegetable?" I ask.

"Shh, don't think of that," my fiancé and his mom say.

His mom suddenly starts nattering about what a good person my mother is, so sweet, going to church.

Where did going to church get her? Lying comatose while surgeons dig around in her skull to stop the swelling and maybe, just maybe, get her to wake up. I try to read one of the nameless consumer magazines piled on an end table, but my attention span is lower than that of an addict on speed.

If you let her just wake up and be okay, able to get around, I'll… I'll… I try to bargain with God.

You'll what, Sharon? You don't want to be a nursemaid. You're 22 and that's not happily ever after.

No, God, conscience, whatever, that's not really it. If only I had woken up earlier and caught her when she drifted off, if I'd acted sooner, if I'd called an ambulance immediately and got her into the hospital right away after I got up and found her…

If… If… if… if "guilt" were one of the seven deadly sins, I'd score 100 plus on it.

"Your mother is resting peacefully." The nurse, June's replacement on the next shift, enters the waiting room. One of the surgeons is with her.

"Your mother is in Intensive Care, still unconscious," he says. "We stopped the swelling, but the next few days will tell. She had a brain aneurysm."

I can only nod.

"Would you like to see her?" the nurse asks.

I nod again.

"I have to get her chart, so I'll meet you over by the elevator."

"Okay," I say.

My fiancé and his mother decide to wait downstairs for me. I tread alone to the elevator. A security guard who thinks he is Chief of Police holds out his arm between the elevator door and me.

"Visiting hours are over," he says.

"But my mom just had surgery. The nurse said. . ."

"It's okay. She's with me."

The nurse has rejoined me and we take the elevator up to Intensive Care.

ICU is like an open room with glass walls. Years later when I roam the halls of George Brown College trying to find the classroom where I will teach, the half glass walls of some of the rooms will remind me of this ICU. Except George Brown's rooms are brightly lit and Intensive Care has a grey sleepy atmosphere, not the relaxed good night sleep, but sleep, hospital style, with IV tubes on stands like sentinels around each bed and everyone in the beds out on meds or their disease. Mom is in a coma and nobody, but God knows if she will wake up, and He's not telling.

My godmother drives down from the farm and Aunt Minnie buses up from Detroit. The former takes over, washing Mom's soiled bed linen and nightgown and draping them on a wooden clotheshorse on the balcony. I start to come out of my shock, at least to call some of Mom's friends and the church to pray for Mom at Mass. I go in to work. What else can I do? Mom's two sisters spend the days at the hospital and I take the subway to St. Mike's right from work. The doctor has moved Mom from Intensive Care into a semi-private, but she stays in a coma, and we seem to have hit a lull. My godmother decides to drive home for a few days to make sure her family and farm are running smoothly, although she says she froze leftovers and the girls can cook. Minnie stays until the next day and then she decides she will return to Detroit. I go in to work.

I'm there barely an hour when a phone call comes in from one of Mom's church friends, Mrs. Cook, the mother of Mary, the girl who used to walk The Bully and me to kindergarten.

"Sharon, I just called St. Mike's and it doesn't look so good. They're not really saying anything, but when my husband was dying this is the way it was. They didn't phone until after he died. You better get down to the hospital."

I phone home and get Aunt Minnie who is just heading out the door. We agree to meet in mother's room at the hospital. Then I receive permission to leave from the Acting Superintendent who says to get one of the staff to drive me. I look around for a cop—preferably a hunk in uniform who can challenge the security guard at the hospital. It is before visiting hours start at 11 a.m. and I don't have enough nerve or body to muscle my way in.

The only cop is a 19-year-old cadet. But Robert is tall and in uniform. He drives me. When we arrive, I ask him to accompany me to the elevator because of the problems with the security guard after hours on Saturday. I feel safe strolling behind this almost-cop in uniform. The guard gives me no problem. I thank Robert and take the elevator up alone. While rounding the bend on mother's floor, I overhear two nurses at their station talking.

"Better phone the daughter."

I rush past them into Mom's room and stop. The sun fills the room with light and whitens the mattress cover of the bed, a direct contrast with the dark oak floor. Leaving the room, I stagger to the nurses' station, managing to tell them who I am.

"I'm so sorry, but your mother has passed away," one of the nurses says. "I'll get the hospital chaplain to talk to you. You can wait in here." She escorts me to a sunroom, as if the sun will bring my mother back to life.

The priest, who has the jagged puffy face of a middle-aged cop, has to tell me what happens next. An autopsy will be performed; that's standard in the early 1970s; then my mother's body can be released to the undertaker. I don't know if I give him the name of the undertaker. I do know that when he asked if there was anything he could do to help, I didn't say, "Find out why they didn't decide to phone me until after she died." Instead I do my usual coward act and shake my head. Aunt Minnie soon arrives. She says she phoned my godmother, and she will return tomorrow.

Back home, I leap into organizing mode, as if with her last breath Mom infused me with some of her qualities. Grabbing her address book, I begin phoning relatives, friends, and the family doctor. My fiancé accompanies me to the funeral home—the same one Daddy's body lay around in. This time I have to make the arrangements and get my first taste of living on credit. You would think while dealing with the emotions from Mom dying, my mind would have no room to worry about money. But the front left block of the brain marked "worry compartment" runs in fast mode, slowing down only when the reality of her death and its aftermath creeps in—such as when the funeral director takes me into Dracula's Shopping Centre, a small room with low ceilings and coffins crammed into rows.

The director does the coffin tour, ascending style. He sweeps his hand through the air over a plain pine board and powder blue coffins and before I can say, "yes," "no," or "maybe," he moves on to the varnished wood.

These luxurious coffins smell like the comfort of an old church. The $735 cost gets buried somewhere between the director's smooth talk and my feelings of guilt. I may have messed up when Mom died, but I'm going to do her funeral right if it kills my bank account. However, I am both my mother's and father's daughter and somehow manage to stay in the middle with the cost.

Somewhere amid phone calls and coffins I step down the street from the apartment to the church office and arrange the funeral. Something else connected to money occurs—Mom's CN widow's pension cheque for August arrives just after she dies.

My godmother takes me to Mom's bank, a TD branch.

"Just fill in the deposit slip in your mother's name and deposit the whole amount in her account," my godmother says. "Don't even tell them she's dead. You can do that in a few days when the cheque clears the bank."

I hold my breath, keep my mouth shut and pass the deposit slip (copy made for my records) to the teller. As she looks at it, I imagine someone, God, my conscience personified, but definitely not Mom, shouting in the teller's ear.

"Julia Langevin is dead."

The teller rubber stamps the cheque and the deposit slips, gives me one, and puts her copy and the cheque in her drawer. Silently she deposits the cheque into Mom's account.

The cheque clears. Of course the estate lawyer has to notify CN of her death. CN writes back instructing me to return the cheque if it hasn't already been processed.

The days following Mom's death are a blur of relatives hurrying in from Detroit, Wasaga Beach, Lucknow, Stratford, Teeswater and Walkerton. Many of them camp out in the two-bedroom apartment Mom and I shared—three bedrooms at night if you count the living room chesterfield that splits in the middle as a bed. The fold-up cot, complete with its mattress gets hauled in from the storage unit across the corridor and plunked in the middle of the living room, and a couple extra cousins share my room which has a double bed and a couch.

Over at the funeral parlour, the embalmer has dressed Mom's body tastefully in her purple dress and pinched, powdered and stuffed her face to try and hide her scleroderma cheeks, and then laid her out in the coffin. So, I have no choice but to play host. I comb my long straight hair, put on my black-with-the-white-striped edge hot pants and mini dress, and stand inside the room greeting guests.

The Bully doesn't show up, but her parents do. Probably, like me at work, they received a phone call from Mrs. Cook. By then, or so I have heard, The Bully's marriage at 20 to a 33-year-old farmer is not doing well and there I am, newly engaged, fiancé with me, and I have lost all my baby fat. But worse, I have now lost both parents. At least The Bully still has her mom and dad.

Second and third cousins living in Toronto show up—including the parents of a second cousin my age I had hung around with at age eight. The mother here yaks a little of this and a little of that, prompting my fiancé to comment, "She's the shallowest person I've ever met."

Aunt Gretchen in a new straw hat, flowered dress, and old yellow teeth shows up with Uncle Theodore for the funeral. The Stratford crowd—my godfather, Aunt Jan, and their oldest children—are along for the funeral, as are most of the Michigan gang. Early Saturday morning, August 7, we drive from the funeral home to the church. The hearse car carrying the immediate family is like a Black Maria minus the police grill. The grey interior reeks of impending death by smothering from the floral arrangements and wreaths along for the short ride to Holy Cross Church. As we file up towards the front pews, I notice Mom's close friends, the Moores, near the back and nod at them.

Once seated in the quiet, I can now worry about whether I should receive Holy Communion. As I am now a non-practicing Catholic who hasn't seen the inside of a confessional since the conscience/sin debate, I also don't do Mass or Communion. Sharon, get a grip, I think. Just file up with everyone else to Communion. But God or the conscience on my shoulder is shouting in my ear.

"But, you haven't been to Confession and if you've committed a mortal sin, you will compound it by going to Communion."

"Yeah, but all my family are practicing Catholics. If I don't go to Communion, what will they think?"

There I go, thinking of me again, and Mom isn't yet buried.

When the priest comes out and does his "look at the bereaved" performance, I decide. No way am I going near the church sanctuary. This priest is liable to grab me by the arm and place me in front of everyone and again shout, "Look at the bereaved."

And I sure needed looking into, but *I* had to do it.

However, first I got married.

24: The Road Most Travelled

New Roads; new ruts

—**Gilbert K. Chesterton**

In the wake of Mom's death, my fiancé and I decide to move the wedding up six months to November 1971. We had already booked the church, and Mom had reserved the reception place. Even my fiancé's birth certificate arrived safely from Burma. So we only have to change the dates, and the rest would be a waltz up the aisle. Maybe…if we didn't decide to make the new date November 13. It wasn't a Friday so what could go wrong?

Apparently, anything. Because Mr. Murphy, he of Murphy's Law, blew in from the netherworld of the Universe and took over. Almost anything that could go wrong, did.

One Saturday morning, I call the restaurant to change the reception date from May 6, 1972 to November 13, 1971.

"We don't have you booked for May 6, 1972. What did you say your name was?"

"Sharon Langevin. L-a-n-g-e-v-i-n."

"Just a minute and I'll double-check."

"Sorry," she says, when she returns. "Can't seem to find it. November 13 is already booked, anyway."

I start to panic. What are we going to do? Maybe we should make it November 20. Do I have to pull out the big guns, i.e., use my connections? I grew up down the street from the nephew of the owner. I decide to try something else first.

"My late mother paid a deposit of $20," I say.

"What was her name?"

"Langevin, Julia Langevin."

She excuses herself to check again. As I listen to the dead air, worry builds inside my head and speeds down to my heart. Where else can we have the reception? I haven't a clue.

"It's okay," the lady on the other end says. "Because your mother already paid the deposit, we can accommodate you. We'll move you up to Saturday, November 13 in our dining room, same price and do you want the same time?"

"Yes. Thank you."

I hang up. Is this a sign of what is to come?

What doesn't come is the money from my mother's estate, not until the following April, a little too late to pay for a wedding.

"We have to cut the guest list," my fiancé says. "We want to invite just those we're close to."

We peruse the list of potential guests finer than a fine-tooth comb, and I make a terrible discovery. He has many friends from University and work. I have four: Ellen, a pal from out west; Sheila, a girl I've chummed with since we met at Shaw Business College; Andrea, the civilian I hang around with at the police department where we work; Sarah, a woman 10 years older than me. I choose only two friends—Ellen and Sheila. But I have cousins, apparently too many cousins. That's where we slice the guest list.

I take my invisible knife and cut out *all* my Dad's relatives. Am I remembering how my aunt neglected to tell my mother the date of another aunt-in-law's funeral? But I like that aunt—we share something besides blood. She and I are both short and I remember one of her favourite expressions, "Why did the good Lord make me so short?" And I love her gravelly voice.

So what is my problem? I am not crazy about her husband, however, the two are a couple, albeit an odd couple. They seem to suit each other, but I am still too immature to get it. I forget my other aunt, Daddy's older sister, she with the big breasts and friendly wicked sense of humour. I forget my dad's older brother and his son and daughters—the latter are old enough to be my uncle and aunts. Besides I only see them at funerals and I'm getting married, not dying.

I tell myself the issue consists of numbers coupled with the lack of money. It is out of my control, so I have to hope for the best. Besides they probably won't know until after the wedding. Too bad I don't think of a compromise, i.e., the number of guess attending a wedding ceremony in a church isn't based on a head count and can be invited separately than those also invited to the reception afterwards. Mr. Murphy is also ignored.

So, my fiancé and I move onto the next items of the wedding planning business:—the invitations (despite no live mother or father of the bride to request "the favour of your presence"), the photographer, and the rings. Surprisingly, all three tasks go well, although the third one isn't your traditional walk into the jewellery store and choose the ring. Some friends of my fiancé are jewellers, and we meet them for dinner. In between the wine and the steak, they haul out sample rings and I try a few on before deciding. Even my gown is no big deal. I stride into a high-class wedding boutique on Bloor Street near work, try on a few dresses, choose one, and proceed to have it altered, including the cape and veil. My wedding will be my moment, so I will dress the way I want.

However, with my bridesmaids and the groom's attendants, I do a 180-degree turn. These are other folks, so I let them choose. My godmother is sewing the dresses for the two bridesmaids—her two eldest, Margaret and Linda. As for the groom's men, their attire will be revealed closer to the wedding day.

So I go on my merry wedding-planning way, never considering how the individual wedding preparations are connected. Mr. Murphy is also still ignored.

After work, I stop at the local flower shop to order our bouquets.

"What colour are your bridesmaids' dresses?" the florist asks.

Dress colour?

"I don't know," I reply. "My aunt is making them."

"We need to have a fabric swatch to match the flowers with."

"Oh."

She asks when the wedding is and shows me sample pictures of fall arrangements.

I write my godmother and ask how the dresses are coming along. She is slow to reply and when she does I don't get the swatch—just a short note that she is busy making them. But she does give me their colour.

"The dresses are brown and green flowered," I tell the florist when I drop in again.

"Do you have a fabric swatch?" she asks.

"No. My aunt is making the dresses."

She must think the situation strange and maybe that I'm peculiar because I don't even know what my own bridesmaids are wearing. *It's their dresses*, I want to shout. I hate it when the bride lords it over her bridesmaids, ordering them what to wear, what style, what colour, and they end up looking hideous and ridiculous. The dresses get ditched later because they aren't something you would wear ever again, except maybe for Halloween. Never mind what happens with my dress afterwards; the wedding day is important.

As it turns out, it is not the bridesmaids' dresses, but the best man and other male attendants' attires that I should be checking.

Meantime, I run into the bakery next door to order my wedding cake. That goes without a hitch, but I don't get a pre-wedding sample of real mouth-watering cake. Instead, I stare at more photos and try to absorb the two-tier or three-tier setup, dark or light fruitcake. I just want cake, finally ordering a small two-tier fruitcake—light—smothered in white icing. At least I am shopping local, so if necessary I can walk the flowers and cake home—placed in my late mother's bundle buggy, of course.

At work, during break, some of the other police clerks and I compare wedding notes. Gwen, who had married a couple of years before, describes her wedding, right from sniffling all the way up the church aisle, honking into a handkerchief at the altar, and the fiasco over the forgotten rings. Of course, none of those mishaps—or any other for that matter—will happen on my wedding day. Again, Mr. Murphy doesn't enter into my planning picture.

When I arrive home that night, I write my aunt-godmother another letter asking, "Where is the fabric swatch?" The wedding is in November, not August or September. I live in an apartment and don't have access to a garden at any time of the year for bouquet flowers.

Meantime, my husband-to-be reserves our train tickets for our two-day honeymoon in Montreal, but doesn't pick them up. We put a wedding announcement in the daily newspapers. The wedding invitation replies trickle in—the only two girlfriends I invited decline and I begin to wonder if maybe we should have invited at least one set of cousins and aunt and uncle on Daddy's side of the family.

The fabric swatches arrive in the mail. Brown, yellow and green flowered, more green than anything else. I take them up to the florist and can finally pick out my bouquets.

One week before the wedding the phone rings.

"So, you're getting married next Saturday," Aunt Marion says. "I saw the announcement in the newspaper."

Oh. Oh. Now I'm in for it.

But she is kind now and I'm feeling a little guilty so I invite her, Uncle Monty and Auntie Clare to the wedding ceremony, at least. They would come anyway.

My fiancé reveals what his best man and assistant are each wearing. I cringe, especially at the best man's outfit—a black velvet suit. At least, my bridesmaids will match each other…and the flowers.

The flowers arrive and I pick up the cake. The rings are safe, and we can get our hands on them in a second. My section at work holds a little pre-wedding reception, complete with cake and a present. More gifts, including two from Daddy's sisters, start arriving at my apartment. So, do my two bridesmaid cousins and my godmother the night before.

Early morning, November 13, the four of us walk the few blocks to the beauty shop formerly owned by another first cousin once removed.

The new owner-hairdresser first washes and curls my long hair, then does the same for my cousins. Their mother had fixed her own short bob before leaving home. Then we return to the apartment to get dressed. We take it in turns to shower in the bathroom. As I fly out of the bathroom and into my bedroom, more and more relatives stop by to check in before going to Holy Cross Church down the road.

But my uncle, my godfather who is supposed to drive the bridal party to the church and give me away, has still not arrived. I glance from clock to watch to clock. Should we lift up our skirts and stroll over to the church? It is so close I can see it from the apartment living room window. However, the wedding party parading down the street midday on a Saturday in mid-November will stop cars just as I trip over my skirt. We decide to wait.

I continue my clock/watch staring and add the apartment door to my surveillance. Finally, at five minutes after the wedding time of 1 p.m. my uncle buzzes downstairs. He has dropped his wife and children at the church and has come to pick us up. The four of us take the elevator downstairs, climb into his car, and are off.

But he doesn't drive to the front door of the church. My uncle takes a detour onto a side street and around a few blocks near the church.

Where ARE we going? Did somebody move the wedding location and forget to tell the bride? My uncle finally slows down and parks the car right in front of the church. We go inside and the ceremony begins.

I would later wonder if all these shenanigans were some sort of sign that marriage is more than a piece of wedding cake. Marriage is a journey— not all uphill, but certainly not an easy slide into happiness with the fairy-tale ending like in the movies I loved to watch. A marriage bumps, lurches, sways, tangos and missteps. It is also harmony, satisfaction, restfulness, and togetherness. But most of all, it is a fluctuating learning curve that continues from the "I do's" to death... if you are lucky. All these hassles and hazards that occurred in the wedding preparation, including why we moved the wedding up six months, should have rung warning bells inside my head.

And perhaps the most important reason to ponder: Daddy and Mom weren't there in person, although their spirits probably were.

Wedding Card from Sharon's Godmother and Family

Epilogue

The hardest thing to learn in life is which bridge to cross and which bridge to burn.
—**David Russell**

If I thought the house at 139 should have protected me from harm, what about all the places my husband and I called home: from finishing Mom's apartment lease to moving to a smaller apartment down the hall, to that first home, ownership of a townhouse in the north end of Toronto, to moving out of the city to a detached suburban house in a town called Aurora?

But I was the daughter of two elderly parents who tried their best, but died before I was fully formed as an adult. The lessons I learned as an only child left me on that damned teeter-totter in this playground called life. It would take me years to learn that life is a learning journey and you can only try to do your best.

And I am still trying.

Mom, Daddy, and Sharon at Her Godmother's Farm

Acknowledgements

I would like to thank the many relatives who helped me over the last 18 years in the extensive research for my memoir. Thanks to my late godfather, who told me stories of growing up in Bruce county, Ontario in my mother's time, and the many cousins who expanded my memories of visiting on the farms in Huron County, Ontario, as well as in Detroit, Michigan. Special thanks to the cousins who took me on tombstone tours to find family graves, and the two cousins who helped me find my Grandpa's farm and meet its owners in 2004.

Thanks to old school friends who continue to share memories of our school years during the 1950s and early to mid-1960s.

Thanks to the librarians in the Walkerton and Goderich Public libraries who steered me towards background history and helped me use the micro fiche machine. Thanks to the City of Toronto Archives, the Archives of Ontario, Toronto Reference Library and various Toronto library branches for articles and books on past area events. Special thanks to the Toronto public library branches who gave me the opportunity to teach Memoir Writing Workshops and Courses.

Special thanks to researcher Deborah Stiff for her extensive hunt for information about a timekeeper's job in the 1950s, and the retired timekeeper she found who explained it all. This helped me understand my father's CNR job and also his and my obsession with time.

Special thanks to Ken McGoogan, award-winning author of *Fatal Passage*, *Lady Franklin's Revenge*, *How the Scots Invented Canada*, etc. Ken's week-long Narrative Non-fiction workshop in 2005 taught me how to blend Canadian history with my story. He also picked apart a chapter in a one-on-one critique.

Thanks to Vivien Fellegi who read an earlier version sent to my publisher and commented from a reader's perspective. Her suggestions helped me with my next rewrite. Thanks to my East End Writers' Group who critiqued various chapters at our meetings, and to Heliconian Club Literature Group members who provided valuable feedback on a particularly stubborn chapter.

And special thanks to Shane Joseph, my publisher for all his valuable editing, criticism and suggestions; some of the latter two go back to 2007, before Blue Denim Press existed. Shane read my memoir's earliest version and said I needed to choose its intended audience from the content of family history, rural Ontario history, and personal odyssey. This started me on the first big overhaul of my memoir. Also, for his support to finally finish this latest version.

Last, but not least, my immediate family – past and present – my late Mom and Daddy, who by just being their unique selves brought both joy and sadness to my life. You will always be remembered as the two people who influenced me greatly; my Grandpa Charlie, for trying to teach me to play Crokinole. And thanks and appreciation to my son, Martin Crawford and his partner, Juni Bimm, for their support, not only with all the computer and camera issues, but being there and listening to me rant.

Author Bio

Sharon A. Crawford is the M and M author. Her Beyond mystery series and memoir *The Enemies Within Us* are rooted in places where she lived. Sharon was born in Toronto, Ontario, and dwelt there most of her life, excluding a slight deviation to Aurora, Ontario from 1975 to 1998 when she returned to Toronto, settling near her childhood home. Aurora (and nearby city, Newmarket) loosely combine as the fictional Thurston in her Beyond mysteries, with Cooks Region and Cooks Regional Police inspired by York Region and York Regional Police. Sharon holds her mother partially responsible for her mystery-writing penchant, thanks to Mom getting her hooked on the old black and white *Perry Mason* TV series during the late 1950s/early 1960s. *Perry Mason* also plays a role in Sharon's memoir *The Enemies Within Us* as that TV series became the arguing point with her Daddy over whether he watched *Hockey Night in Canada* or Mom and Sharon watched *Perry Mason*. Mother and daughter usually won. However, Sharon's previous career as a secretary, particularly with an Aurora law firm and Toronto Police Services definitely added to her desire to write mysteries. Toronto is also where Sharon's childhood was shattered by her Daddy's cancer, which is recounted in *The Enemies Within Us*.

A former journalist for 35 years, Sharon currently runs the East End Writers' Group, belongs to Crime Writers of Canada, Sisters in Crime, and the Toronto Heliconian Club. She is a freelance editor and teaches short story and memoir writing workshops. She also hosts *Crime Beat Confidential* on thatchannel.com. Sharon spends her spare time walking in her neighbourhood, pulling weeds and harvesting vegetables and fruit in her garden, reading mystery and memoir, watching TV, or chatting with her son, cousins, and friends on Facebook, Zoom and telephone.

www.ingramcontent.com/pod-product-compliance
Lightning Source LLC
Chambersburg PA
CBHW072004110526
44592CB00012B/1195